Equipped To Win!

JimSundberg.com

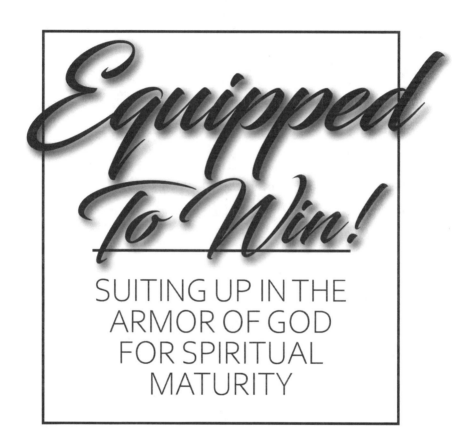

Equipped To Win!

SUITING UP IN THE ARMOR OF GOD FOR SPIRITUAL MATURITY

JIM SUNDBERG

3X ALL-STAR, 1985 WORLD SERIES CHAMPION,
6X GOLD GLOVE AWARD WINNER, TEXAS RANGERS HALL OF FAME

EQUIPPED TO WIN!
Suiting Up in The Armor of God for Spiritual Maturity

© 2022 Jim Sundberg.

ISBN (Print Edition): 978-0-9993652-3-6

ISBN (Kindle Edition): 978-0-9993652-4-3

Library of Congress Control Number (LCCN): 2022912642

Printed in the United States of America

Published by Sundberg Leadership Team | Arlington, Texas

Edited by Wendy K. Walters | wendykwalters.com

Prepared for publication by | palmtreeproductions.com

Scripture Copyright Information:

To contact the author:
JIMSUNDBERG.COM

Dedication

To my amazing wife, Janet—for your love, faithfulness, dedication, and support for over 50 years of marriage. You have been the love of my life since first meeting you when you were just 15.

To our children, Aaron, Audra, and Briana—you are walking out your faith in Christ with your sent-from-God mates, Cari, Chuck, and Stefon. Thank you for giving us ten wonderful grandchildren.

— • • • —

Acknowledgement

I wish to express my gratitude to Wendy Walters— my comrade in arms on this project. Thank you for your vision and brilliance in editing my work.

*"Do you not know that those
who run in a race all run, but
only one receives the prize?*

*Run in such a way that
you may win."*

1 CORINTHIANS 9:24, NASB

Contents

FOREWORD BY DR. JACK GRAHAM   1

INTRODUCTION   3

FUNDAMENTALS OF SPIRITUAL MATURITY 7

     THE ROLE OF PROTECTIVE ARMOR   9

     A GOD OF ORDER AND UNITY   13

     THE BATTLE BETWEEN GOOD AND EVIL   17

     OBJECTIVES OF EACH ARMOR PIECE   31

FOUNDATIONS FOR BATTLE 33

     BELT OF TRUTH   35

     BREASTPLATE OF RIGHTEOUSNESS   59

KINGDOM BUILDING 91

     READY SHOES   93

     SHIELD OF FAITH   125

SEASONED WARRIORS 155

     HELMET OF SALVATION   157

     SWORD OF THE SPIRIT   185

EQUIPPED TO WIN! 211

     KEEP ON PRAYING   213

     PERSONAL WORKSHEETS   221

. . . .

     RESOURCES FROM JIM SUNDBERG   229

Foreword

Baseball is a game I have loved pretty much my entire life. It is a classic game that demands skill at every level. Running. Throwing. Catching. Fielding. Hitting. Perhaps the most demanding talent on the playing field is the catcher's position. The player behind the plate calling and receiving every pitch. Managing the field. Working with pitchers' mental attitude. Keeping the umpire happy and in the strike zone. Squatting up and down 150 plus times a game, catching a variety of fast balls, breaking pitches, taking balls in the dirt, foul balls in the face, and a variety of other body parts. Being a catcher is challenging and even dangerous at times. For this reason, the catcher's gear is absolutely essential.

No one knows this better than my good friend Jim Sundberg who caught nearly 2,000 games in the major leagues and was an all-star with my beloved Texas Rangers and a world Champion with the Kansas City Royals. A Gold Glove catcher, team leader, and clutch hitter, Jim played at the heights of baseball stardom. He is a member of the Texas Rangers Baseball Hall of Fame and a leader in the Dallas Fort Worth community. Jim is, above all, a committed veteran follower of Jesus. He loves God's Word and lives it.

You hold in your hand a unique and inspiring book. It's all about winning battles. Not baseball battles but spiritual battles which believers face every day.

Using the catcher's equipment to illustrate the spiritual armor we must all put on to win the battles of life and eternity, Jim prepares Christ-followers for the warfare.

Equipped to Win is a gripping explanation of the biblical principles God has given us in Ephesians 6 that our faith will stand against the enemy's attacks. I have long admired Jim's ability to communicate God's Word through the power of personal stories and the testimony of his own walk and witness for Christ.

I can hardly think of a more important subject in our generation and for the generations that follow than spiritual warfare. As we approach the end of the age, we must prepare ourselves and our children for a ferocious and furious fight. God has promised provision and protection, but we must wake up, stand up and gear up to live a victorious life. Paul says, "we are more than conquerors"[1] and "if God be for us, who can be against us?"[2] And in the end, we know the "God of peace shall soon crush Satan under our feet."[3] But until then, we are to fight the good fight and never give up or give into the seductive strategies of Satan.

Read this book. Devour it. Underscore and mark it up because in it, you will discover your game plan for life. As we put on "God's gear" every day, we will not only be protected in battle but will take it to our adversary and all his demon forces and defeat every enemy and satanic stronghold in Jesus' holy and powerful name.

—*Dr. Jack Graham*

Senior Pastor, Prestonwood Baptist Church

ENDNOTES

1. Romans 8:37.
2. Romans 8:31.
3. Romans 16:20.

WARM-UP

Early in my major league career, I learned about an elite group of men whose stories dramatically influenced my life. In the 1920s, these power brokers collectively controlled more money than the United States Treasury. Entire generations have been influenced by the keys to success these millionaires practiced, and still today, many parents hope their children grow up to achieve even a fraction of such wealth. What I learned, however, were the tragic shortcomings and failures of these idealized leaders.

As president of Bethlehem Steel, Charles Schwab built a personal fortune worth $25 million but was forced to borrow money during the last five years of his life and died penniless. Richard Whitney, president of the New York Stock Exchange, served time in Sing Sing prison. Albert Fall, a member of Warren G. Harding's cabinet, was given a pardon from prison so he could die at home. Jesse Livermore, the fabled "bear" of Wall Street, committed suicide. Ivar Kruger, the owner of a worldwide monopoly, and Leon Frazier, president of the Bank of International Settlement, also killed themselves.

How ironic and tragic that these mighty men would lose it all in the end! Why couldn't they sustain the success that brought them to the heights of power? What fatal flaw would cause their lives and empires to implode? Their haunting tales of ultimate power and ultimate failure astounded me as I was on my own fast track to success. Their stories helped to change my perspective and goals.

There seems to be little difference between those involved in church and those with no religious affiliation. Too many pastors and leaders have been led down a pathway of adultery, financial misconduct, and destruction, resulting in families and congregations left in shock. Many leave the church either for another place of worship or are so deeply wounded by the situation that they abandon organized religion altogether. Tragically, some walk away from their faith completely. Leaders should know good from evil; they should know God's voice and learn to discern and judge righteously. What does it mean if those we should be able to look to as mentors and models fail so often? Is there any hope for the "regular" person?

Life is a spiritual battle. We are constantly being transformed—changed either by the renewing of our mind or its depravity. We do not stand still. We grow mature or embrace immaturity, not physically but spiritually. Just as there is emotional intelligence and financial intelligence, spiritual intelligence exists, and it can only be discovered as it is lived out. We must utilize our will as the vehicle for seeking the Lord's will. We must become like Jesus, who clearly stated, "I do what My Father does."

There is a real enemy in this world that is out to steal, kill, and destroy. This enemy wants to drive us to walk in fear with a weakened defense system that leaves us vulnerable and weak in our spiritual life. Our fight is not against flesh and blood, although the enemy clearly uses the souls and flesh of men to cause great harm to people.

As I observed those around me in baseball, I saw similarities with the industrialist-era power brokers. As in high finance, Major League Baseball offers a quick rise to fame, extremely high salaries, and glamorous perks, followed by a steady, private descent into obscurity. Could my own aspirations to succeed cripple my long-term dreams? The answer is YES. It could, and it did. I began to wonder how to avoid the pitfalls that had trapped the mightiest of men.

I realized early on that I needed to be proactive in finding the answers before they found me. My biggest challenge was that I tend to want things **now**. But growing into an accomplished major league professional baseball player takes years of learning, adjusting, repetition and practice. The same is true of our spiritual maturity and wholeness. And maturity is not determined by the number of years one claims they are a true believer in Christ but rather the amount of time and discipline it would take to understand who He is correctly and embrace the spiritual life and wisdom He is leading us towards.

Although I had grown up in the church, it took the tremendous pressures of a high-profile sports career for me to realize I needed Jesus Christ in my life. My first three years as a Christian had its challenges. While I did not read the Bible on a daily basis, what I did read, I had trouble discerning. I struggled to distinguish between a heavenly Father of unconditional love and my own earthly father for whom I couldn't please or do well enough. My hurts and wounds kept getting in the way of my spiritual development towards maturity and wholeness.

———————————— • ● • ————————————

The conditional patterns developed during my childhood made me distant from my heavenly Father's love for me.

———————————— • ● • ————————————

Paul wrote the book of Ephesians while imprisoned in Rome. Rather than address any particular problems in the church, Paul wrote this epistle to explain some of the great themes and doctrines of the Christian faith. He concludes the book with instructions to put on the full armor of God and stand in spiritual maturity. I will explore this "armor of God" concept in-depth in this book.

The enemy of our soul seeks to inflict fear that will cause us to withdraw from God and not fulfill our destiny. The Armor of God is there for our protection and to defend our personal freedom in our pursuit to be all that God intended. Applying the truths of the Armor of God becomes a way of life, making one equipped for spiritual maturity.

I've discovered that interesting parallels can be made between my major league catching gear and the equipment Paul outlines in Ephesians 6 for the biblical armor. I do not think it is a coincidence that I wore the tools of a catcher for so many years and then became so moved by the application of the spiritual version. I have sensed a calling to write this document. I will expound on the concepts of each piece of armor which I believe give us the freedom to live in spiritual maturity. I will use the New Testament as a backdrop for understanding the deeper precepts while drawing parallels to my experience in major league baseball. The armor pieces are concepts given to go deeper and further in our spiritual maturity. I pray that God will open up your heart to its deeper truths and that this text will honor God and this work of grace and love in my life.

—*Jim Sundberg*
Arlington, Texas

Fundamentals in Spiritual Maturity

EQUIPPED TO WIN!

THE ROLE OF PROTECTIVE ARMOR

ar·mor—1) defensive covering for the body (especially used in combat), 2) a quality or circumstance that affords protection, 3) a protective outer layer.[1]

When the fighting was over, a Roman soldier could peel off his protective armor and set it to the side until another conflict. The same is true for the Major League catcher as he leaves the stadium after the competition. He can take off his protective gear and leave it behind. Neither the soldier nor the ball player has to wear or carry all the pieces all the time. For the Christian, though, it is different. The Armor of God is more like a second skin. It is always with you. God's protective armor needs to become the window through which a Christian views life. The armor contains all the necessary tools to live a victorious life for Christ.

While in prison, Paul realized that the armor worn by Roman soldiers offered protection only for the front side. There was no armor for the back of the soldier. The design itself conveys that Romans confronted their foes and never backed away. There was no plan or preparation for retreat. Paul models the Armor of God after that of the Roman soldier, indicating that in spiritual warfare, a Christian is to take the offense—never backing down—but always moving forward in their fight.

In this study of the Armor of God, do not become intimidated or overwhelmed. Fighting spiritual warfare effectively can come down to a consistent study of the Word, a disciplined prayer life, and the daily expression of joy and thanksgiving through praise and worship to God. The enemy of this world cannot deal with those elements. Even if you do not understand how each piece of the armor works or how to make the appropriate application, as a believer, you can easily utilize the tools just mentioned.

Over time, you will come to understand each armor piece and how to use it. The Word of God, a disciplined prayer life, and songs of praise will be a great companion during this period of learning. Through our study, you will grow in your understanding of the fundamentals of Christianity. The Armor of God can be looked at as a way to develop spiritual maturity for followers of Christ.

This book is a study in spiritual maturity that encompasses the basics of Christianity and leads you on a journey to wholeness. We will explore:

- Our relationship with Christ,
- Intimacy with God,
- Application of the truth of God's Word as it applies to His saints,
- The power of prayer,
- The basic doctrines of the gospel of justification,
- Reconciliation,
- Propitiation and regeneration,
- Love,
- Forgiveness,
- Repentance,

- Grace, mercy, and peace,

- Witnessing to the lost,

- Joining God in service to others,

- Faith and trust amid hardship and conflict,

- Submission to God and its disciplines,

- Sacrifice,

- The process of right choices and the consequences of wrong ones,

- … and more.

This manuscript was first presented in early 2000 to a publisher, and after a few levels of acceptance, it was rejected at the last minute on its final review. The mindset I took from the rejection is that, for some reason, God was not allowing it to go forward, and I was okay with that. Perhaps it needed more work, or maybe I was not yet spiritually mature enough to handle what might come my way from writing a text of this nature. For whatever reason, fifteen years later, I have been moved to pick this project up and finish it. I am grateful for the additional wisdom and knowledge I have gained over the last dozen years and, therefore, glad I did not publish this work earlier.

Since I first began writing this book until now, I have been moved by the Holy Spirit's presence and insight. No man has a corner on the truth. We know what God has chosen to reveal to us, and that is known through the filter of our flesh—experiences, beliefs, faults, and all. So, I invite you to test everything in this document with Holy Spirit. It's astonishing to write something I felt so inadequate to explain. It's in God's presence, though, His empowering grace, that I am qualified.

ENDNOTE

1. Armor. Definition from www.merriam-webster.com/dictionary/armor. Retrieved 02/15/2022.

---•●•---

It is in a life of discipline that we truly find the riches this life has to offer. As we develop spiritual maturity, one day, we will realize the extent of our riches for eternity.

---•●•---

A GOD OF ORDER
AND UNITY

Over the course of eternity, God has shown Himself to be the omniscient (all-knowing), omnipresent (always with us), and omnipotent (all-powerful) guide for us in the world. He exists as the Triune God, mysteriously three in One: God the Father, God the Son (Jesus), and God the Holy Spirit. Through these distinct personalities, God accomplishes all that He is to us, has for us, and wants for us.

Ever since the beginning of His creation, God has worked in succession. He separated the land from the sea and provided every life form with everything they needed for sustenance. He ordered the days from one to seven, allowing time for every task necessary for life. Night and day and the cycles of seasons provide the basis for time and ecology. God created the human body to function so completely and efficiently that science has yet to develop even a modest substitute for its complexity.

In the fullness of time and because of mankind's sinfulness, God provided a holy substitute for our unrighteousness—His Son, Jesus Christ. Christ came into this world and died for our sins so we could be reconciled to the Father. Jesus did this according to God's promises to His people and the lineage of Old Testament saints.

On and on, throughout the Bible and in our own individual lives, God is consistent in why, how, and when He works. Having understood that God is a God of order and unity and that everything He does or creates has meaning and purpose, I believe that a distinct correlation exists between how the individual pieces of armor are ordered and united in Ephesians 6 and how we are to apply them in our lives.

Much of the book of Ephesians talks about unity—unity of the body and the Spirit of God united as one. The armor pieces are also biblical concepts of order and unity given by Paul. These allow us some flexibility to expound on the fullness of their meaning and ways to utilize and apply them. Behind each piece of armor, we find a richness of content to be applied in daily life for spiritual maturity. You will come to discover how valuable God's armor is in the healing of wounds and the freedom brought by that healing process. As you understand the deeper meaning of the armor pieces and navigate the pathway ahead, you will grow in spiritual maturity and wholeness.

In my journey, I have discovered that one piece of armor has a tendency to build on the next, with each successive piece interrelating with the other. Just as learning numbers leads to the concept of counting, then addition and subtraction, then later on multiplication and division, then finally higher mathematics. In this same way, the pieces of God's armor are the fundamental building blocks we must comprehend to move into the depths, breadths, and heights God means for us to explore in Him.

God has given me a skill set to join Him in bringing a sense of order and definition to concepts. In that same context of order, I see where the Armor of God gives us a sense of direction as it communicates its message to us. This study has proven to be an indescribable blessing. It is a joy and privilege to join Him in this work and even help others experience Him.

May this labor of love and discipline reflect God's calling on my life over the last forty-plus years, and may I glorify Him by living up to the high calling of discipline in my own life. I want this book to serve as a testimony of how God has changed my life. I share some personal testimony of events in my life with you, hoping it will release you to pursue a higher level in your relationship with Christ. I also want to encourage you to be brave and daring in sharing your stories with others and become a model to others as others have been a model to me.

THE BATTLE BETWEEN
GOOD AND EVIL

I was at a Promise Keepers event in Dallas many years ago and heard a great local preacher, Dr. Tony Evans, comment about spiritual warfare. He communicated to the audience of over 40,000 men that God and Satan have moved and counter-moved against each other since the creation. Tony gave details of how that had occurred throughout scripture and how it would continue until the appointed time in the future.

The following are tidbits of some of the encounters between God and Satan that Dr. Evans outlined in his speech and his book, *The Battle is the Lord's*. These points provide a reference point for the foundation for spiritual warfare we will explore.

- ***God made the first move in this cosmic contest when He created the world, including the entire angelic host.***

- *Satan countered that move by rebelling and taking a third of the angels with him in his rebellion.*

- ***God answered Satan's rebellion by creating Adam— His new representative to rule over the earth.***

- *Then Satan tempted Adam and Eve to rebel against the authority of God.*

- **God provided redemption for Adam and Eve so they could be brought back into fellowship with God.**

- *Satan tried to counter that move by getting Cain to kill his brother Abel to cut off the godly line.*

- **However, God reintroduced the godly line through the birth of Seth.**

- *Not to be outdone, Satan's next counter-move was to lead the entire world into rebellion against God.*

- **Oh, but God had another counter-move to make. He found a righteous man named Noah and commanded him to build a boat, providing salvation for a family and wiping out the rest of the world.**

- *So Satan found his own man, Nimrod, and tempted him and his friends to build a kingdom in an attempt to be independent of God, a move that led to the judgment of the tower of Babel.*

- **That's when God made a brilliant counter-move, going to Ur of the Chaldeans, to call a man named Abraham and send him to Canaan to become the father of a righteous nation.**

- *Satan countered God's move by causing Israel to become enslaved in Egypt.*

- **God sent Moses to Egypt to tell Pharaoh, "Let my people go."**

- *Satan tried to pin Israel against the Red Sea so the Egyptian army would destroy them.*

- ***But God countered Satan's move by opening and closing the Red Sea at the right time.***

- *... and the battle wages on ...*

Dr. Evans goes on to say, "That's the way it was throughout the Old Testament. That the coming of Jesus Christ was God's greatest move in this spiritual 'chess game' called spiritual warfare. Jesus decisively defeated Satan for all of time and eternity and stripped the devil of his power."

I think you get the picture of what the scriptures are trying to say about this battle of good and evil that has raged between God and the devil since before creation.

Just as the saints of the Old and New Testaments had to endure these struggles from the heavenly realm, so do the saints of today (believers) have to rely on God to win their battles. Whether these struggles come right into our own homes in the form of alcoholism, drugs, and sexual abuse, abortion, adultery, and strife between others—Christian-to-Christian, Christian to non-Christian, or godly governments against godless authorities—the same is true: spiritual warfare is real for all. Only in our relationship with God can this battle be understood, confronted, and won.

I read a phrase years ago in a text, *The Complete Biblical Library*, that made this statement about spiritual warfare: "This battle is real, difficult, and dangerous. Although salvation is free to the person who receives it, it is not culminated ultimately without great effort. No true soldier of Jesus Christ can expect to be immune from the assaults of the enemy, and no Christian can afford to be neutral in the conflict."

WHY IS SPIRITUAL WARFARE
IMPORTANT TO ACKNOWLEDGE?

THE ENEMY MOVES WITH STEALTH

If we look behind the scenes of the September 2001 bombings of the World Trade Center and the Pentagon, we can see some similarities in this difficult and dangerous battle between good and evil. We will be able to pick out several key elements suggesting that evil comes in under disguise with the intent to do harm. Much like a soldier in battle who needs to stand his ground to survive, so does the Christian need to be aware of what is going on around them so that, when the day of evil comes, they can respond appropriately.

The evil perpetrators of the 9-11 attack came into the country under stealth. They got their visas, the government lost track of them, and they blended into neighborhoods and communities without anyone appearing to have recognized anything abnormal. They used the freedoms of this great country to take advantage of the areas where we were vulnerable. They knew where our weak points existed in this free society. They used our resources to educate themselves enough to fly a highly technical and sophisticated aircraft. We granted them easy access to ride on our aircraft—planes with a system that tolerated easy entry into a private cockpit area.

The dark forces of this world in the spiritual realm will use the same types of strategies to gain access and entry into our lives.

They can come in under secrecy, not wanting us to know they are there. Using our vulnerabilities, they will gradually try to move us down a road of compromise and then toward destruction. Without realizing their presence and evil intent, we may actually aid them in their cause. Through our lack of knowledge and understanding about ourselves and the way they work to deceive, the enemy of our soul gains easy access to personal areas of our lives. Unwittingly, we open the door by our spiritual blindness caused by our self-centeredness and lack of spiritual discipline.

YOU CANNOT ADDRESS WHAT YOU WILL NOT ACKNOWLEDGE

When I was playing for the Texas Rangers in the early '80s, a situation developed that would eventually be used to discredit me as a catcher and later in getting me traded to another franchise. In my early years as a catcher, there were not many ways an adversary could find to de-value me. A catcher is eventually graded on three areas of work—defense, offense, and game calling. I got to the big leagues because of my good defense, and it was hard to find anything to criticize. People usually do not come after you on that strength when you are the best at something.

I struggled hitting the first several years, but while one is considered a "budding star," people would say, "That's okay, he is here because of his defense, and he is learning to hit while he is in the majors, leave him alone!" I did eventually start hitting, and by the summer of 1978, I made it to the cover page of *The Sporting News* with the title, "Best Backstop?"

By the time I was moving into the middle years of my career, the Rangers had made many transactions that brought new players, new coaches, and new front office people to Arlington, Texas. The team was struggling and not doing well, so people started pointing fingers, looking for someone to blame. Up until now, I had avoided being accused as the reason for the team's dismal showing or downfall. But this time, the hammer started to drop in my direction.

I was great at defense; I was much improved at hitting, so the only other way a catcher is judged is by game calling. I had thus far been excused in this area, too, partly because I was young and partly because

I had played for Billy Martin. Anybody who spent time around Billy Martin *knew* the trauma he brought upon the catcher.

Billy was the biggest second guesser in the history of baseball. If a hitter hit the ball, according to Billy, it was the wrong pitch. He used to say, "Jim, if you get in a situation with the winning or tying run in scoring position and want to know what to call, just look over here, and I will signal you with the right pitch." So, when we would get in a close game situation, I would look over to the bench to get the signal from Billy. However, he always seemed to be getting a drink of water and wouldn't look at me. Well, I think you get the picture.

So for years, upper management left me alone when it came to game calling. When I say they left me alone, that's what I mean. I didn't get criticized, but I also didn't get any help. I had to learn as I went, and looking back, I admit that calling games was the last thing that came together to complete me as a catcher.

Someone, though, at this point, thought that I should be better at calling a game. I'm not sure where it started, but before too long, that I should be better at it had widespread endorsement among the pitching staff. I caught wind of it on the front end, with the whispers, but I would not acknowledge its existence. I thought it was just foolish talk and irresponsible for pitchers to blame a catcher. A part of me said I should confront it, but no one did such a thing in the baseball culture. It was better to gossip and make excuses for your own mistakes rather than take responsibility by confronting them. So I went on, downplaying the issue, not wanting to acknowledge that it

Before you can solve a problem, you must first acknowledge its presence.

22

was true. So my credibility was gradually undermined, and two years later, I was traded.

For example, everyone knows (except the alcoholic) that before they can be helped, they must first admit, "I'm an alcoholic." In the same likeness, the only way to fight and win against the spiritual forces in the heavens is to acknowledge that spiritual warfare does exist and it is real.

Whatever denomination a person associates with is often an indicator of how serious that person will address the concept of spiritual warfare. Some denominations go to one side and say that everything is demonic without taking personal responsibility for their condition. They do not acknowledge that a situation could be caused by free will choices, sin, or that it may even be God. On the other hand, in some denominations, people become afraid of the possible reality of a spiritual battle. Afraid and ill-equipped for what to do, they would rather not acknowledge its presence.

So if we can get to this point of believing in the existence of spiritual warfare and find a healthy balance, then the next step is to understand how it works. With that understanding, we can determine the best approach in fighting the battle.

HOW DO WE TACKLE SPIRITUAL WARFARE?

PURSUE BALANCE

Theologian C.S Lewis says that the devil loves two types of people; the skeptic and the superstitious. The skeptic doesn't believe Satan exists, and the superstitious believes there is a demon behind every bush. One camp doesn't even want to acknowledge the possibility of a spiritual enemy, and the other blames everything on the devil. These are both great deceptions requiring us to seek balance by moving toward the middle.

Before discussing what the middle looks like, let's briefly reference the importance of acknowledging the devil's existence again. Many outside the church do not believe in spiritual warfare. The thought for the skeptic is, "Since I don't believe in God, there is really no reason to believe in the devil." A person who believes in evil generally knows that God exists. It's hard even to imagine that any Bible-believing person who has read the Gospels would not believe in an adversary. But there are still many in this category. On the other side of the spectrum is the superstitious, who believe there is a demon around every corner. In this category, a person becomes obsessed with the idea of Satan and his demons. There is a tendency to avoid thinking that a struggle is of the flesh—our sin nature— or that God might be doing a work in the believer through a trial. For clear understanding, in this book, I have taken the position that a believer cannot have a demon living inside them. They cannot be *possessed*. However, a believer can mindfully be under demonic influence due to unreconciled issues where the enemy had an investment in the original wound. They can be *oppressed*.

What does this mean?

Wounds are entry points or open doors for the enemy. He is always up to "no good," causing havoc in all directions. Demons are dreadful beings. Satan is out to kill, steal, and destroy. Any form of evil, destruction, or abuse has his signature of approval. Therefore the enemy is the original shareholder of every form of wrong-doing that only Jesus can cure or defeat.

God is in control of all things.

We are God's workmanship and sealed by the Holy Spirit (Ephesians 2:10), but that doesn't keep the enemy from influencing our lives. As mentioned, wounds and offenses are entry points—open doors for the enemy—because he most likely had an investment in the original sin, a wound he perpetrated through another. If we stay wounded, we remain under the enemy's influence. More will be discussed later in the text.

To seek balance and move toward the middle, a believer needs to ask Holy Spirit to give them the gift of discernment in this area of spiritual warfare. You must genuinely seek truth here to avoid having your emotions mislead you. You must seek wisdom to understand when, how, and why the enemy is attacking you. This book plans to help answer those questions.

Scripture suggests we walk in balance when it comes to understanding spiritual warfare. We must be careful about blaming what on whom. The best strategy requires wisdom and discernment. ***We must ask Holy Spirit:***

> 1. *"Is this from the evil one?"*
>
> 2. *"Is it from our basic nature?"*
>
> 3. *"Or is it of God?"*

Paul often talks about the internal struggle between the old nature and the new one.[1] Yet, while it is not smart to ignore Satan (the skeptic), it is also not wise to go to the other side of the spectrum and overemphasize the work of the devil (the superstitious).

I like word studies. When I checked, the words "Satan" and "Devil" appear seventy-eight times in the scriptures. When I put in the words "Jesus," "Lord," "God," and "Spirit," the computer kicked out eleven thousand, six hundred and sixty-one words! That calculates into a 150 to 1 ratio. That's one hundred and fifty words representing our Lord, God, and Savior to every one word used to describe the adversary. Wouldn't it be wise and helpful to be aware of this when choosing our words as we seek balance?

BELIEVE IN JESUS

> "Our struggle is not against flesh and blood (people),
> but against the rulers, against the authorities,
> against the powers of this dark world and against
> the spiritual forces in the heavenly realms."
>
> EPHESIANS 6:12, NIV

We first need an advocate in the spiritual realm that carries a big punch. Without knowing Jesus as Lord and Savior, spiritual armor is of no use.

Jesus' death on the cross and His victory over the devil is the only thing that has enough power for us to win the struggle against such strong forces of evil. When Jesus spilled His blood at Calvary, it gave us the ultimate weapon to fight the enemy. It put Christians in a position of authority, power, and strength to come up against the adversary in "the Name of Jesus" and win. Once we know our source of power for the battle, we can examine where the vulnerabilities and the easy access points exist against us.

UNDERSTAND YOURSELF AND THE ENEMY

By understanding yourself, you can better put into play a discipline that will keep you from aiding the enemy. As a ballplayer, when I came to the realization of a flaw in my swing, I would step up to the plate in the batting cage, as a discipline, to work out the flaw. Then, what was once an entry point or easy access area for a pitcher to defeat me, now became something for me to manage. I took the responsibility to take appropriate action to block the pitcher's strategy.

Know areas where you have been wounded or still carry an offense. These are entry points and areas of easy access for the enemy to steal, kill, and destroy your destiny. They are usually situations that have caused anger, fear, or pain, often in childhood, but they can also be in your recent past. Unreconciled areas of our lives, arrogance, and pride are a breeding ground for the enemy to hassle us and cause mass confusion. The enemy works to deceive us through these areas of vulnerability. I will give you more detail on how this works in chapter two, under the Breastplate of Righteousness.

KNOW THE DIFFERENCE BETWEEN SPIRITUAL WARFARE AND A SPIRITUAL BATTLE

When addressing the idea of a spiritual attack, there are several things to consider before discerning where the conflict is coming from. You must be able to filter through the three possibilities—the enemy coming against us, our flesh wrestling with a character issue, or God working to conform us to Christ's image—before deciding on the plan for defense. ***Whatever the case, God has allowed it, and He will work it for your greater good.***[2]

Whether you face spiritual warfare with the enemy or a spiritual battle within your soul, God can use it for your spiritual maturity.

The believer can approach it this way:

- Is the conflict I'm experiencing coming from an outside source?

- Is the enemy of this world harassing me, or is the source of agitation coming from within?

- Is my flesh doing battle with my spirit?

- Is the battle coming from some other kind of influence?

27

- Do I have a blind spot I need to address, and
  God is trying to get my attention?

Over the years, in my struggle to understand this battle, I have misdiagnosed some of my own conflicts. I have also seen others who didn't want to take responsibility for their conflict, so it went unresolved. It sat there beneath the surface, waiting to come back again when the right set of circumstances converged.

Far too often, we give the enemy credit for something that is of our own flesh nature. We do not want to think that God is in the process of developing our character or consider the possibility that the conflict we are experiencing might be the loving discipline of the Lord.

It is extremely important to recognize that spiritual warfare and spiritual battles are real and difficult. We must filter this understanding through truth.

Not all conflict is warfare. Many come from our relationships, our

---●●●---

Properly identifying the source of our struggle is paramount in determining the right strategy that will be used to resolve

---●●●---

GROW IN YOUR UNDERSTANDING AND EXPERIENCE

For a new believer or for someone who has never before engaged in spiritual warfare, it can be a challenge. Lack of knowledge and proper application of the armor can result in being in a state of defense—on your back, swinging at the air, hassled continuously, which could be overwhelming. But even a few steps of growth can make all the difference. A consistent study of the Word, a meaningful prayer life, and the daily expression of joy and thanksgiving through praise and worship to God will help greatly and lead you to victory.

Knowing the pieces of the armor and how to use them daily is a preventive action to stay on top of whatever comes your way. A seasoned warrior knows how to wear the armor to deflect the enemy's fiery darts.

The image of a Roman soldier in battle is compelling. He had no armor on his backside.

Do you want to stand and fight, confronting your opponent, or do you want to fight while lying on the ground, looking up, fighting feverishly for your life?

This book will coach you on developing a winning strategy for fighting the good fight of faith.

Understanding your entry points will give you a proactive way to fight offensively rather than always on the defense. Let's get started!

ENDNOTES

1. See Romans 7:15-20.
2. See Romans 8:18-30.

OBJECTIVES FOR EACH ARMOR PIECE

At the beginning of each chapter, I will provide these key objectives:

WHAT DOES THIS ARMOR PIECE MEAN?

I summarize a clear description of what truth this armor piece represents to our spiritual life.

WHY IS THIS ARMOR PIECE IMPORTANT?

Understanding the purpose of each piece is the real motivator in challenging us to become better skilled in learning and applying the piece of armor

HOW DO I "PUT ON" THIS PIECE OF ARMOR?

An explanation of how we "put on" the intended piece of armor will provide a practical application for the spiritual discipline.

WHAT RESULT CAN I EXPECT FROM APPLYING THIS ARMOR PIECE?

For each piece of armor, I provide a two-word "action result" that comes from the proper application of the armor piece.

WHAT ARE THE ENEMY'S TACTICS?

*For each piece of armor, I warn you of the approach your soul's enemy will use to try to deceive you in this area. It highlights **why** you need the protection of the armor.*

WHAT ROLE DOES APPLYING THIS PIECE OF ARMOR PLAY IN SPIRITUAL MATURITY?

I will summarize what key points you can expect from each chapter, and the spiritual blessings which result from the proper application of the armor.

"Finally, be strong in the Lord and in His mighty power.

Put on the **FULL ARMOR OF GOD**, so that you
can take your stand against the devil's schemes.

For our struggle is not against flesh and blood, but
against the rulers, against the authorities, against
the powers of this dark world and against the
spiritual forces of evil in the heavenly realms.

Therefore, put on the full armor of God, so that when the day
of evil comes, you may be able to
STAND YOUR GROUND, and after you
have done everything, to stand.

Stand firm then, with the **BELT OF TRUTH**
buckled around your waist, with the
BREASTPLATE OF RIGHTEOUNSESS in place,
and with your feet fitted with readiness that comes
from the Gospel of Peace (**READY SHOES**).

In addition to all this, take up the
SHIELD OF FAITH, with which you can extinguish
all the flaming arrows of the evil one.

Take the **HELMET OF SALVATION** and the
SWORD OF THE SPIRIT, which is the Word of God.

And pray in the Spirit on all occassion with all kinds of
prayers and requests. With this in mind, be alert and
ALWAYS KEEP ON PRAYING for all the Lord's people."

EPHESIANS 6:10-18, NIV

Foundations for Battle

THE BELT OF TRUTH

THE BREASTPLATE OF RIGHTEOUSNESS

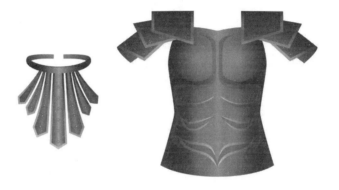

Any successful endeavor or concept has a set of principles that lay a strong foundation for its future success. In baseball, developing the skills for hitting, fielding, throwing, and base running become the foundational elements needed to become an effective baseball player. More directly, your passion, hard work, skills, and discipline become key ingredients for any successful endeavor.

The Belt of Truth and the Breastplate of Righteousness are the foundational elements of our spiritual maturity and wholeness. They are the fundamentals that allow us to wear all the other pieces of armor. Until you master how these first two work, you cannot effectively utilize the rest of the armor.

As Christians, our potential to grow and mature will rest on how well we understand and apply these foundational concepts. Our willingness to struggle with the pursuit of these elements will rest on our continuous pursuit of God and His power, through the Holy Spirit, to intercede and guide us along this path. Many will never experience the greater advantages of being in an intimate relationship with Christ because of our fear of engaging and wrestling with truth and righteousness.

If we are willing to embrace our relationship with Jesus, who is Truth (the Belt), and understand His deep love for us (the Breastplate), it will set us free to do amazing things for the Kingdom of God. These armor pieces will establish a foundation in Christ that will lead us into experiencing the joyful and abundant life that the Word of God talks about and that Christ wants for us.

Chapter One
BELT OF TRUTH

WHAT DOES THE BELT OF TRUTH MEAN?

Jesus is our starting place and the foundation for all truth.

WHY IS THE BELT OF TRUTH IMPORTANT?

Truth holds together all the pieces of armor.

HOW DO I "PUT ON" THE BELT OF TRUTH?

I put on the Belt of Truth by pursuing intimacy with the Father—shooting straight with Jesus.

WHAT TWO-WORD RESULT CAN I EXPECT FOR APPLYING THE BELT OF TRUTH?

Set Free

WHAT ARE THE ENEMY'S TACTICS?

The enemy puts a spin on truth through deceit and lying.

WHAT ROLE DOES APPLYING THE BELT OF TRUTH PLAY IN SPIRITUAL MATURITY?

- *Impacts your relationship with Jesus*
- *Deepens your intimacy with God*
- *Unlocks the Truth that will set you free*
- *Gives you the freedom to shoot straight with God—the safety to be fully known*
- *Empowers you to acknowledge emotions*
- *Helps you listen to Holy Spirit*
- *Uncovers the enemy's tactics*

BELT: STARTING POINT

ALL-STAR CHAPEL

On the day of the 1995 Major League All-Star Game in Arlington, Texas, I was asked to be the speaker for the event's annual breakfast with the All-Star players. My topic was the Armor of God, and I had put on my old baseball uniform to demonstrate the different pieces of "armor" with my catcher's gear. Because I would be using it as a demonstration, I hadn't put on my uniform's belt, and I didn't really think much about it. However, the late Texas Rangers manager Johnny Oates saw me without my belt. "Where's your belt, Sundberg? How come you don't have it on?" he playfully demanded.

Leave it to the manager to recognize when a player is not in full uniform! Until the belt is securely fastened, players are not in full uniform, and they're not allowed on the field. They are not ready for competition until the belt is in place. To a Christian, the Belt of Truth is just as important. We cannot expect to be ready for the battle ahead unless we stand in the truth and pursue it, in an almost reckless abandonment of everything else.

The Belt of Truth is first in the Ephesians passage because it is the foundational piece that the rest of the armor pieces depend on for their function. Until the belt is fastened, you are not ready for battle. Truth is like water to a thirsty soul; you can't leave home without it.

In Roman times, the belt or girdle was wide and served multiple functions as it held the entire outfit together. It helped anchor the breastplate with a tight fit, leaving no room for arrows or knives to penetrate. In the same way, the Belt of Truth brings additional support to the next piece of armor (the Breastplate of Righteousness).

EASE OF ACCESS

In baseball, being a better player starts in practice. If you want to improve your swing, you head to the batting cage to work out the so-called "kinks in your armor." The player may look at adjusting his swing, and his ultimate desire is that through repeated exercise and muscle memory being established, these fundamentals will transfer over into the game.

In the spiritual realm, the practice time for putting on our Belt of Truth can start in the morning in our quiet time with God. In the Old Testament, only the high priest was allowed into the Most Holy Place at certain times of the year, where God dwelled. When Jesus died on the cross, however, the veil that separated the Most Holy Place from the Holy Place was torn in half, representing that anyone who believed in Jesus could now enter into an intimate place with God.[1] Because of Christ, we can now fearlessly approach God to commune with Him.[2]

INTIMACY: PERSONAL RELATIONSHIP

In sixteen years as an MLB player, I went through 18 managerial changes and played for two of the managers twice. For the longest time, I didn't know where the role of the manager fit nor had much respect for many. I did not see good character examples or good leadership with most. Then I was traded to the Kansas City Royals in 1985 and played for Dick Howser. Everything shifted in experiencing what a good manager should look like.

Dick Howser was amazing to play under; respected, smart, consistent, and steady. He gave me confidence in managers again. The year we won the World Series, Dick only called for two team meetings that lasted no longer than 20 seconds each. Basically, he said we were playing hard, hang in there, and things will turn in our favor. And sure enough, things turned around halfway through the '85 season. We came from seven games back of California at the All-Star break to win our division and advance in the post-season to win it all.

Before the trade to Kansas City, Dick had made a public comment that made me want to play for him. In an interview, he told a sportswriter, "If we (KC) got Jim Sundberg to work with our young pitching staff, we'd win the World Series." Wow! I hadn't heard such respect for some time. It made me want to be a better player and play as hard as I could.

The previous three years had been difficult. My one year in Milwaukee in '84 had been a good stopover before KC, but the last two years in Texas with the Rangers were rough as my star began to fade after ten years.

I almost didn't make it to KC in '85, though, due to a disagreement among Royals ownership. As told to me later through the lens of the Royals comptroller, here is how the story went.

The meeting consisted of the Royals' two owners, Ewing Kauffman and Avron Fogelman, and the brilliant general manager John Schuerholz, along with the KC comptroller.

As a side note, Schuerholtz went on after his stint in KC to be the general manager for the Atlanta Braves from 1990 to 2007, where his teams won 16 division championships in 18 years. Afterward, John served as President of the Braves from 2008 to 2016. He now serves on the board for the Atlanta Braves. Schuerholz was inducted into the Baseball Hall of Fame in 2017.

As the story goes, Schuerholtz went to the ownership to discuss trading KC youngster Don Slaught and picking up veteran catcher Jim Sundberg from Milwaukee to handle a young talented pitching staff consisting of Brett Saberhagan, Danny Jackson, and Mark Gubicza, along with veterans Charlie Leibrant and Bud Black. Great pitchers make smart catchers, and I ended up with a great staff.

Fogelman responded negatively to the idea of the trade, stating that he would like to keep the younger player Slaught over trading for the older catcher Sundberg. The conversation went back and forth for some time until the meeting broke up, and Schuerholtz vacated the room. That left the two owners and the comptroller still in the room together.

With Schuerholtz gone, Kaughman turned to Fogelman and said, "Who wants to do it?"

Fogelman countered, "Do what?"

Kaughman said, "Fire Schuerholtz!"

"Why in the world would we fire John?" responded Fogelman.

"We don't." reacted Kaughman, then added, "why don't we let him do his job!"

So, I got traded to the Royals in January of '85 and experienced a World Championship that fall.

The next season started out rough, and by mid-season, we were not doing well. Dick made a mound visit to take out a pitcher during a Sunday afternoon game before the All-Star break. I looked at him and remarked, "You look tired. Dick."

The skipper responded, "I do feel tired, and I haven't been feeling well." That's all the conversation we had before the new pitcher arrived and Dick left the mound for the dugout.

Dick was to be the manager of the All-Star team that year in 1986, as historically set by MLB. Whoever the managers were in the previous World Series, they would be the two managers for the next season's All-Star game. Whitey Herzog was the skipper for the National League.

Three days after Dick's Sunday mound trip and one day after the Tuesday All-Star game, Dick collapsed to the ground. Upon being taken to the hospital and with further tests, it was determined that Howser had an aggressive brain cancer that would be difficult to treat. Dick would never return to the field and passed away in the summer of 1987.

Several weeks after Howser's collapse in 1986, he invited me over to his house for a visit. I didn't know what to expect, but he blew me away. After some small talk about the team he said, "Jim, there is something different about you; what is it?"

Wow, where do I go with this, I thought. Then after a short pause, I shared my faith with him.

Dick sat quietly and listened very intently. It was an amazing time to share with a great man I deeply respected as a baseball mind and one I had become very fond of. He commented about my humility and other affirming things—I had come a long way.

The crazy thing is that I didn't even know I was being watched. I wasn't even aware that by the way I carried myself, I was having an influence. I naturally thought I was lacking in some areas and in need of God's grace. I wasn't perfect, I made mistakes, yet God used me that day.

I may have been brought to the Royals for the young pitching staff, but the more obvious reason was that God had greater things in store. Dick eventually became a believer in Jesus as his Lord and Savior before he passed away.

I grew up in the church and religiously went every week through high school. I went because I had to go, my parents made sure of it. Later on, I was thankful for that. But I really wasn't into going to church. Years later, in 1977, I accepted Jesus into my life as Lord and Savior in a hotel room in Toronto while reading Hal Lindsey's book, *The Late Great Planet Earth*. I learned that there was a Heavenly Father who loved me and could handle anything I could dish out without being critical or judgmental. He accepted me the way I was and wanted a relationship with me. No religion—just a loving relationship.

A friend once told me that religion is sitting in church while thinking about fishing. Relationship is thinking about Jesus while sitting in your boat fishing.

The bottom line for all truth and the basis for which all things are established is that "Jesus is the way, the truth, and the life. No one comes to the Father but by Him. If you do not know Jesus, you do not know the father!"[3]

EMOTIONS

ACKNOWLEDGING FEELINGS

I grew up believing that sharing intimate things with another was off-limits. Having a Swedish background, my ancestors were very private people. I had an uncle who had a very difficult time losing an infant child, as anyone would. Knowing the Sundberg heritage, it had to be tough on Uncle Dale to share. I remember my dad criticizing his brother privately at home while he struggled with his loss. My dad's comments communicated to me not to share anything with anyone.

Then in 1980, I attended a professional athletes conference in San Bernardino, California, where Campus Crusade for Christ used to set up its headquarters. Some three years after becoming a Christian, I went there to do some soul searching. At this conference, I would hear a man share with a small group of ten couples that would forever re-shape my thinking about vulnerability.

See, I went there all tied up in knots. I had been emotionally holding things inside for years. I was really hurting and went there to look for a breakthrough in my young Christian faith. Previously, I had been led to think that if you shared something intimate in a group, you were a weak person. By the time this tall, masculine, All-Pro NFL football player got through talking, I was in tears. How gentle, wonderful and courageous his testimony came across. I believe the Lord sent me there to hear a model of strength and manhood share such a touching story in an attempt to open me up emotionally to others.

After this event in California and seeing the value of relationships, I knew I had to do something else. So I sought counseling. Another no-no with my dad, but I pursued it anyway. In fact, today, most MLB teams have staff counselors on hand for players. Over the years, I've had many counseling sessions to get at the root of my childhood wounds.

I'll never forget one of my first counseling sessions when the counselor, during an exchange, asked, "Well, how did that make you feel?"

I froze. Unsure how to answer. *Feelings? What are those?* I was programmed to be an athlete, and feelings weren't part of the checklist. I asked the counselor if he could give me an example. He said, "Well, if that happened to me," referring to an incident, "I would feel sad." As soon as I heard that word, I broke down and started crying. I learned to connect with sad for the first time, well into my twenties.

Addressing feelings is critical to spiritual maturity.

— • ● • —

If you understand your feelings,
acknowledge those feelings,
and ask yourself questions,
it will lead to a more healthy place.

— • ● • —

VULNERABILITY MATTERS

I had to learn to be more comfortable in my own skin while being vulnerable and have the security of heart to open up to others. It's not easy, as Larry Crabb describes in his book, *Silence of Adam*. He said this:

> *Men are easily threatened. And whenever a man is threatened he becomes uncomfortable in places within himself that he does not understand, he naturally retreats into an arena of comfort or competence, or he dominates someone or something in order to feel powerful. Men refuse to feel the paralyzing and humbling horror of uncertainty, a horror that could drive them to trust, a horror that could release in them the power to deeply give themselves in relationship. As a result, most men feel close to no one, especially not to God, and no one feels close to them.*

Vulnerability is not an easy subject to enter and scary for one attempting to break free and expose something personal to another. Vulnerability is a state of openness of the heart, communicating a wound, concern, or hurt to others. It's being authentic with who you are and what's going on with your heart. When the stresses and anxiety of life hit, it's healthy to share those in the safety of trusted family members or friends.

I realize some people are not safe to be around. I'm not talking about pursuing those relationships. Some relationships will never be healthy to engage in. I'm also aware that a certain amount of discernment is needed on what to share, to whom, and when to share.

I'm thankful that my pathway of courage took me through a window of vulnerability to be emotionally open with others. There is freedom in doing so. Public speaking aided my openness. It wasn't until about the age of twenty-six, though, when sharing with others started, six years into my marriage.

I'm now involved in a men's event called Quest. During this six-day event, men are observed opening up in front of a group, and we watch life changes occur. It's very rewarding to see men walk away with greater freedom and healing over their lives. God does amazing things when we are courageous enough to share our emotions with Him and then unmask those feelings with others.

In his book *Wild at Heart*, John Eldridge says, "men suffer in silence." Secrecy and emotional isolation are killers! I like the phrase, "Isolation is the darkroom where you develop your negatives." I'm not sure who said it, but it's brilliant. The enemy of this world works in this setting. I can't tell you how many stories I've heard of well-intended, Bible-reading people who ended up in a bad spot. When stuff happens, do you run toward God or run from Him? The sequence is this:

- something bad happens

- guilt and condemnation follow

- your self-image deteriorates

- you isolate, keeping secrets from God and others

- then disaster

It pays to stay connected and involved in relationships. At the moment of first damage, re-engage with safe people—the quicker, the better. Isolation and hiding create an open door for the enemy to wrap lies around your identity, which will block you from God.

Two abuses in my childhood kept me locked in a private world well into my young adult years, which I will talk about in the next chapter. These incidents caused me to lock up and be trapped. The amount of anxiety that occurs while keeping something locked inside is enormous.

Proverbs says a "wise man has many counselors."[4] King David said, "When I kept silent, my bones wasted away through my groaning all day long."[5] David was a man after God's own heart and ended up shooting straight with God. David had been wasting away by holding back and keeping things locked up inside. Vulnerability is the pathway to emotional stability and spiritual maturity. Period.

I felt much like King David in my early years of baseball, as I kept silent with my wounds. Wounds can come in a number of ways; lost relationships, a health crisis or traumatic injury, childhood abuse, divorce, marital problems, death of a close loved one, job issues, and so on. Being open with others is the pathway to emotional health and freedom, even if, at times, the truth can hurt.

In the movie, *A Few Good Men*, Tom Cruise asks Nicholson for the truth in a courtroom exchange. Nicholson responds, "Truth—you can't handle the truth!" It's a dramatic scene highlighting that truth may sting. There are examples where being truthful may hurt for a short time, but truth leads to freedom and spiritual maturity.

SHOOTING STRAIGHT

What an amazing concept that, as believers in Christ, we can enter into a private audience with the all-powerful God. Something in the Old Testament that was once reserved for a select few is now open for all who believe on His name. Wow! Can you imagine intimacy (in-to-me-see) with a Holy God who actually wants to meet with you and me!

For years in my Christian walk, it was hard for me to believe that I could establish intimacy with God by being vulnerable with Him. Even though I logically knew God could read my thoughts, it was hard to shoot straight with Him (confess my wrongs and have intimate conversations).

Through my earthly dad's model, I had learned to be afraid and grew distant from this loving God. The breakthrough came when I was reading Psalms and read about the life of King David. What really caught my attention was that this man of God, who by far was not perfect, was still considered a man after God's own heart. On further inspection, I discovered that this man was considered a man after God's heart because he "shot straight with God" because God can handle it.

— • • • —

You can tell God absolutely anything. Nothing you can say will shock Him or cause Him to pull away from you.

— • • • —

ANTIDOTE FOR POSING

I hit another growth spurt in the early 90s, about eighteen years into my Christian walk. This season is probably why I am writing this text today. I had come to a crossroads where I thought there was a lack of authenticity and honesty in my faith. I was trying to deal with a bout of depression and could not tell others to pray for me. Basically, pride hindered the process of healing because I didn't want anyone to know I was hurting. I smiled on the outside but was dying on the inside. In addition, some people who thought it was cool to know Jim Sundberg had previously burned me on some less threatening prayer requests by using them as gossip, so my trust was low.

I took a major leap toward spiritual maturity as the concept of shooting straight with God began to change my life. The following confessions eventually liberated me, and as I have shared these over the years, I have found that they are similar to many of you. I pulled these out of my journal during this season of life. The antidote for posing is shooting straight. See if you haven't felt this way at one time.

1. I'm playing Christianity. My walk is not genuine. What people see is not real! Lord, help my walk to be more honest.

2. I use you, Lord. I draw close to You when I hurt; then I go my own way when I feel better. Help me not to dishonor You in that way!

3. Why isn't there more power in my life to overcome bondage? Why do I carry this "old person" around? Help me to see what I'm missing!

4. If I don't learn to know You better, if something doesn't change, I'm not going to make it. I need more of You and less of me! Help me give up control!

5. I don't know what's more powerful in my life: my fear of hell or my love for You! Help me to love You with all my heart!

6. Death scares me. Heaven seems like a fairy tale. Make eternity with You more real to me.

These six confessions are being vulnerable and authentic with the Lord. It is learning to take the lead from the Holy Spirit and then take what He has revealed to you and express it back to Him. If you want to have a heart that is after God's own heart, this exercise is a good start for you.

At the end of this chapter, there are some pages for you to work on "shooting straight" with God. Being vulnerable is one way we apply the Belt of Truth in our life. As we learn to be real with God, this close relationship with the Lord will profoundly change how we seek genuine connections with others and seek truth in this world.

LISTENING TO HOLY SPIRIT

BRILLIANT COUNSELOR

If the most brilliant counselor were living inside you, why wouldn't you want to know Him better? Wouldn't you want to tap into everything He has to offer? It would seem wise to do everything possible to learn to hear when He speaks. There are about twenty references in the Bible to the character and actions of the Holy Spirit; the author of scripture, comforter, counselor, advocate, convicter of sin, deposit, seal, earnest, guide, the indweller of believers, intercessor, revealer, Spirit of Truth, Spirit of God, Lord, Christ, Spirit of Life, teacher, witness.

That's what the Holy Spirit is all about!

Throughout different seasons of counseling, I have tried to put words linking emotions with wounds that needed healing. One of my counselors, a pastor, began to work with me on listening for the Holy Spirit. This was new. It's amazing to have been a Christian for so long and no one had ever taught me what listening to Holy Spirit was all about.

We got out a piece of paper and first wrote, "Dear Lord." I was then instructed to write a concern or prayer down. He coached me to write, "Dearest Jim," and wait to write what I heard. It was tough going at first, but I became better skilled at this exercise over time. I've ended up with many journals from this process. In time, I didn't need to write it out anymore; I could just converse with Him openly without using a journal.

This was a game-changer in counseling. Now I could go directly to the Brilliant Counselor as one method for growing in spiritual maturity. In this exercise, a person brings a hurtful event to God and asks Him, "Where were you this memory?" The following is a small example.

Lord, this abusive incident with my dad was such a hurtful, confusing and scary memory—to be beaten, not for what I did but for what I was thinking! Lord, where were You in that memory?

———————————— • ● ● ————————————

Dearest Jim, I was lying there next to you! I was holding you with My arms wrapped around you! I had ahold of your heart with one hand while holding your neck and head with the other to cushion the blows. I felt every thrust, every hit, and every blow from your dad. Even then, I had a hedge around you! I felt and tasted his wrath. I buffeted you from further damage. I wept with you. I'm so sorry you had to go through that! I was so close your tears rolled across my heart as a future memory of this moment so that I could bring you to complete healing in this season of life. You can grieve it, My son! You are <u>safe</u> with Me now. You didn't do anything wrong; I thought your words were highly creative!

As the words flowed across my heart from Him, I wept with healing tears. When I finally heard Holy Spirit say, "Jim, you didn't do anything wrong; in fact, I thought your words were highly creative," I was healed! The pain from the memory was over. The above dialogue is a small portion of this interaction, and the entire piece took a couple of settings to write, and the writing came after several years of practice. My journaling started out looking much more elementary, but you can see that the response I received from God was loving, tender, and in-depth.

God's responses are always consistent with His Word.

PASSIONATE PURSUIT

I grew up living across from a ballpark in Galesburg, Illinois. I was the first one in the ballpark in the morning and often the last one to leave at night. It was then that I knew what a passionate pursuit of something was all about. I poured my heart, soul, and mind into baseball. I couldn't get enough of it. The same can be true in our relationship with God.

I believe that there is an attitude that the Holy Spirit will develop in the mind and heart of the believer who genuinely pursues Him and His truth. It is a biblical fact, and I can say that I have learned this personally. If you consistently seek Him, you do not have to worry about getting too far off the path of truth.

One of the problems I had during the first part of my life with finding truth is that while I religiously went to church, I went there because my parents made me. (Though I'm thankful for that today.) I did not attend church because of my pursuit of God or His Truth. I just wanted to be a Major League ballplayer, and I didn't have a choice about church.

After being a Christian for more than forty years now, I've seen similar behaviors from others. Children go to church because they, too, are being well guided by their parents but will personally, at some point, have to make a decision on their own. I've seen grown-ups who go to church socially or as a habit without pursuing a personal relationship with God.

My 94-year-old dad told me before his passing that the only reason he went to church was to honor mom because she had a value for it. Others go to church because it would be a good business practice to be seen there. Church attendance void of the wholehearted pursuit of God and His truth is nothing but a legalistic act of attempting to be good. Good doesn't get it in the Kingdom of God.

When we put the Belt of Truth on every morning, we commit to our relationship with Christ first and then with others. We open ourselves to the prodding of the Holy Spirit, allowing Him to correct our course when He brings light to our eyes that we have strayed from any truth. His prodding takes the pressure off of remembering. We don't have to perform or make it a "to do" list for the day with Him. Seeking Jesus—the Truth—becomes a passionate pursuit in a culture where truth is hard to find.

SET FREE

PURSUING JESUS

We cannot know and accept the deeper truths of scripture without knowing Jesus as Savior. We must love and have a deep desire for truth to discover it. If there is any truth in life, it is consistent with scripture. The result of seeking Jesus and discovering truth, even amid difficulty, is that we are set free to experience the abundant life.[6] A subtitle for this book could be "Pursuing God to Become All That He Intended." Spiritual maturity says, "If I walk with God, I have a chance to reach my highest potential. If God is my shield, I have the greatest opportunity to succeed."

I was in the old Soviet Union not long after East Germany's wall was torn down. What surprised me was how depressed the Russian culture was and that you could very easily see it in the eyes of the people. I wondered how we could have ever been so afraid of these people—so down-trodden and sad looking. What caused this to happen? How could this despair reach so many people?

As I spent time there and had discussions with people, it became clear that this was first a society without God, and second, because of the lack of God, personal freedoms were almost non-existent. The more a society removes itself from the one true God, the more it will lose its personal freedoms.

External freedoms are different than internal freedoms. No one can take away the inner freedom you experience in an intimate relationship with Jesus.[7] That freedom allows you to move about in the presence of danger and not be afraid. You can move around and know that God will give you direction every time during trouble, until that last time when He comes to take us to be with Him. And even then, He protects you.

Jesus will hold you. Always. As surely as He is your King of glory, He is also your Prince of Peace. Let this truth comfort you.

ENEMY'S TACTIC

PUTTING A SPIN ON TRUTH (LIAR)

The subtle spin used by the enemy appears to be reserved for the more knowledgeable person as a Christian. In the Gospels, we read the dialogue between Jesus and Satan.[8] Three times, the devil tries to put a subtle spin on the truth of God's Word. Jesus responds with the actual truth of God's Word to counter Satan's master liar craftiness as he twists the verses.[9] This is how Satan will work in the life of a believer. Unknown, he will come, slowly trying to get us to concede what we know to be true, and then if we do, he will look to move us down that road of compromise that could eventually lead us to destruction.

A godly friend once said, "We are in the spiritual realm. It involves battles, campaigns, hand-to-hand combat, victories, losses, and real casualties. It is the real war—earthly wars are only a façade masquerading as this one. It is going on all the time—everywhere. Many Christians are unaware of it and are sleeping or picnicking right on the battlefield!" You must KNOW THE TRUTH and be aware of the enemy's subtle tactics that bring a spin on the truth!

SUMMARY

TRUTH IS FOUNDATIONAL FOR EVERYTHING

The Belt of Truth is a foundational piece that sets the stage for all the other pieces of armor. Discovering truth is a battle worth the pursuit. Truth is a constant theme throughout Paul's discussion of spiritual armor. A relationship with Jesus represents truth, and shooting straight with Him is the starting place for authentic relationship.

Our pursuit of freedom and spiritual maturity is wrapped around this relationship. Finding freedom and growing in spiritual maturity motivates our passionate pursuit of all truth. When truth is applied to the next piece, Breastplate of Righteousness, we find our identity and true significance and experience healing, emotional freedom, and spiritual growth.

STEP UP TO THE PLATE

THE BATTING CAGE

When a baseball player steps up to the plate in the batting cage, he takes responsibility to practice until he gets the desired results. The batting cage is where he goes to practice something that needs work in his swing. The player then takes what he has accomplished in the batting cage and applies it in the batter's box at home plate during the game. He steps up to the plate, taking responsibility for what happens. He can't blame another player, the coach, or even the umpire. It's up to the player to get the results.

In the spiritual realm, it's up to God for the results to the degree we lean into Him. We put ourselves in a position to receive love from God by being mindful of what the Holy Spirit wants us to do.

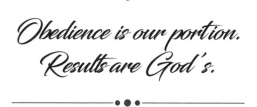

Obedience is our portion.
Results are God's.

Prayer is the most powerful action we can undertake. Prayer aligns us with the Spirit in doing what God sees and wants us to do, His will. In the Garden of Gethsemane, when Jesus was under great duress, He said, "Not my will but Yours, Father!"[10] It's the ultimate alignment with God.

At the end of each chapter, there are exercises designed to help you step up to the plate for your family and yourself, asking the Father to give you "eyes to see" and "ears to hear" as it applies to the content in each section.

REFLECTION

Developing a consistent quiet time is the starting place for putting on the Belt of Truth. Prayer, worship, and a heart of thanksgiving are elements that prepare your heart to receive God's truth. As you find a place to be alone and quiet for this exercise, listen to these two songs and let their words soak into your heart.

- "Give Me Jesus" by Jeremy Camp.

- "Search My Heart" by Hillsong United.

The Armor of God's protection only works for those who have accepted Jesus as Lord and Savior.

1. **Where are you today in your relationship with Christ?**
   Maybe you have already accepted Jesus and started that journey.
   Using the space below, write out your testimony (When,
   where, and any other details that are meaningful to you.):

   Let's begin by shooting straight! Understanding emotions are a
   major part of fighting spiritual warfare because acknowledging our
   feelings aids us in having an intimate and authentic relationship
   with Christ. Anger is usually rooted in fear and has a connecting
   lie. Anger and fear are mentioned many times in scripture as a
   warning. If you can acknowledge anger, you can generally trace
   it to some form of fear. This helps you identify the lie that has
   wrapped itself around this fear so you can replace it with truth.

2. **What is the trigger for your anger?** What is the fear
   behind your anger? What is the lie connected to the
   fear? Now, what is the truth about what God says?

Here is an example:

> **Anger:** My boss just raked me over the coals.
>
> **Fear:** I'm a failure!
>
> **Lie:** I'm not adequate enough.
>
> **Truth:** There is no condemnation for those in Christ!

Now you try!

> **Anger:**
>
>
> **Fear:**
>
>
> **Lie:**
>
>
> **Truth:**

3. In his book *Wild at Heart,* John Eldridge uses "posing " to refer to when we are not honest or authentic with Jesus, others, and ourselves. When we sit posing down and "Shoot Straight" with Jesus, we activate the best way of putting on the Belt of Truth in pursuing an authentic relationship. **Are there any confessions you would like to share with Him?**

56

4. We can take shooting straight one step further and bring healing by confessing to others. James 5:16 instructs us to confess our faults to one another, then pray so we can be healed. **Who do you trust to make this step of faith with?**

5. Jesus said to the Pharisees, "You belong to your father, the devil, and you want to carry out your father's desire. He was a murderer from the beginning, not holding to the truth, for there is no truth in him. When he lies, he speaks his native language, for he is a liar and the father of lies."[11] It doesn't get any clearer than that, does it?

    Several years ago, I was talking to a lady judge who presided over a family court in Dallas, and she made the remark, "It is harder to tell which parent is telling me the truth; people are getting so good at lying." **Is there a lie the enemy generally uses with you? What truth do you need to recognize to counter the lie?** (Use the list below for help.)

    Here is an example:

    > **Lie:** I'm a failure; I don't have what it takes; I'm stupid!
    >
    > **Truth:** I'm loved deeply by Jesus, accepted and approved. I'm chosen by the King of Kings for good works. I have what it takes to succeed.

    Now you try!

    Lie:

    Truth:

6. One way to develop intimacy is by writing letters (journaling) to the Father. This exercise helps us to begin listening for the Holy Spirit. **Do you have any anger, fears, anxiety, or other issues needing prayer?** Write out your prayer to the Father. In response to the prayer, sit quietly and listen. What do you hear?

Dear Lord, (Write your request.)

Dearest (Your Name, Write God's response to you.)

ENDNOTES

1. Matthew 27:51.
2. Ephesians 2:18.
3. John 14:6.
4. Proverbs 15:22.
5. Psalm 32:3.
6. John 10:10.
7. John 8:32.
8. Matthew 4:1-11, Mark 1:12-13.
9. John 8:44.
10. Luke 22:42.
11. John 8:44.

Chapter Two
BREASTPLATE OF RIGHTEOUSNESS

WHAT DOES THE BREASTPLATE OF RIGHTEOUSNESS MEAN?

Our identity and position in Christ are precious, and they must be guarded.

WHY IS IT IMPORTANT?

Once wounded, it is easy to wrap lies around our identity that seem like the truth. The Breastplate of Righteousness is there not only to shield us from the enemy's fiery darts (lies), but also to provide a place of safety and refuge so our wounds can heal as we pursue the path of forgiveness that leads to peace.

HOW DO I "PUT ON" THE BREASTPLATE OF RIGHTEOUSNESS?

When I absorb God's deep love, I put on the Breastplate of Righteousness. This piece of armor protects my heart and reminds me that I am forgiven, approved, accepted, and renewed.

WHAT IS A TWO-WORD RESULT I CAN EXPECT FOR APPLYING THE BREASTPLATE OF RIGHTEOUSNESS?

Restored Heart

WHAT ARE THE ENEMY'S TACTICS?

The enemy disrupts our significance by hindering our ability to receive God's love.

WHAT ROLE DOES APPLYING THE BREASTPLATE OF TRUTH PLAY IN SPIRITUAL MATURITY?

- *Gives me a clear understanding of my identity and position in Christ*
- *Strengthens my core with an understanding of four basic doctrines of Christianity—Justification, Reconciliation, Propitiation, Regeneration*
- *Helps link God's deep love to hurtful experiences*
- *Helps me find significance*
- *Helps me break free from strongholds in my mind*
- *Gives me the strength to persevere, to forgive, and to see the enemy's tactics*

BREASTPLATE: RESCUED HEART

GOOD GOOD FATHER

When I was nine years old and learning to play baseball, I heard that a young person could get hit in the chest with a ball and cause his heart to stop. Being a pitcher and outfielder, it somewhat frightened me to think that I could be hurt bad enough to die. The following year I was asked, first by the coach and then my dad, if I would like to become the catcher. From my short time in sports, I knew that the catcher wore protective gear (the tools of intelligence, I might say). The thought of having something protecting my heart sounded pretty good to me.

Playing baseball over the next thirty years, I was hit countless times in the chest without injury. In my 16 years of Major League Baseball, I made only one trip to the disabled list due to a back injury.

As time went by, I became confident in the safety of my chest protector. Under that security, I broke free from the fear that once tried to keep me from doing what God had intended for me.

In spiritual terms, the Breastplate of Righteousness protects our heart from the enemy's blows whose intentions are to render us helpless to fight a good fight of faith.

God is a good good father. His love knows no bounds. When we understand God's deep love for us, step into who we are in Christ (our identity), and understand our position in Him, we begin to establish spiritual maturity. As we grow, our heart is in a good place to receive everything heaven has to offer.[1]

IDENTITY AND POSITION IN CHRIST

WORLD CHAMPIONS

On the day of the seventh game of the '85 World Series, I took the family to one of Kansas City's beautiful parks to relax to get away from a house full of close family members. It was the most stressful day in my entire career. Wow, Game 7 of the World Series, and in a few hours, one team would be crowned Champions. I had waited my entire life to play in this game, and here it was upon me.

I struggled to be present in the moment as the kids played while sitting next to Janet. I was deep in thoughts about the big game. It was an uncomfortable tension as I thought about the coming night.

Janet suddenly asked, "Where are you?" I told her that I was wrestling with my emotions that were all over the board.

"Janet," I said, "all the previous games have been close, but I feel like this will be a blowout—and the problem is I'm not sure who is going to win!"

The time at the park was nice, and it was a reprieve for me from my father, who so uptight it was hard to bear being in his presence. Dad always wanted to be a big leaguer, and he didn't get that chance; he was a good player in his own right. In a strange way, my dad was acting like he was going to play.

When I got to the ballpark, all the nerves settled down. It's what we were trained to do. All the emotions shifted into a good place as we went about our business getting ready for the game.

Brett Saberhagan was our young star pitcher on the mound that night, and he had his stuff. After catching him in the first inning, I returned to the dug-out and told our manager, Dick Howser, "Brett was so good; if we scored one run, we would win!" It brought a smile to his face.

By the fifth inning, we were up 11-0, which would fulfill my prediction of a blowout—thankfully, with us winning. The last four innings of that game were the most fun ever played; we knew the game was ours, and we started to do some clubhouse celebration away from the crowd (and to make sure our opponent did not observe our early merrymaking). The final score was 11-0 as Saberhagen threw a gem shutout.

As a Christian, I liken the last four innings of that game to being a follower of Christ:

- we knew the championship and title was ours (position),

- so our confidence abounds in the final outcome (eternal security),

- our opponent is defeated (Satan),

- we have no fear of losing (we are sealed),

- we can enjoy our position of strength until the final out (walk in our identity).

- Still, we have an opponent (Satan) who is crafty and good at what he does,

- he wants to take us down, so we must attend to any comeback (persevere).

We step into our identity and position by knowing and believing by faith in the spiritual heritage available to us. Spiritual blessings are a gift that God has lavished upon us, which can be activated at conversion.[2] We have trouble believing in something given to us. Generally, our response is, "What's the catch?" Almost everything we do in life has to be earned. But as a Christian, our identity or position in Christ is given to us. Not so for an MLB player.

An MLB player has numerous assets available he's earned or acquired over time—his equipment, his uniform, his ability, his title, his awards, a voice of credibility at his position, a place of prominence on the team, game experiences, and knowledge of the game.

At conversion, a follower of Christ has every spiritual blessing at their fingertips. We just have to know what the spiritual blessings are, acknowledge those gifts, then start acting by faith that we possess them. Most believers don't know what they have in Christ, so therefore they don't take advantage of what's available. A believer eventually has to step into their identity by acknowledging the spiritual blessings and then activating those blessings (utilizing what's already there) while moving in authority. In other words, spiritual blessings are useless unless we know what they are and act upon them.

HEIRS

As a Christian, you can appreciate the similarities between the 1985 series-ending game and the infinitely more important spiritual race we are running. We are heirs to the Kingdom of God! Christ has paid the penalty for our sins, the evil one has been defeated, and eternity with God is ours. We are <u>royalty</u> and <u>saints</u>! Nothing can take away our identity and position. We just need to press into our understanding of the authority and power that God has already given us!

I like what Paul says about our identity and position in Christ:

> "Praise be to the God and Father of our Lord Jesus Christ, who has blessed us in the heavenly realms with every spiritual blessing in Christ. For He chose us in Him before the creation of the world to be holy and blameless in His sight. In love, He predestined us for adoption to

sonship through Jesus Christ, in accordance with His
pleasure and will—to the praise of His glorious grace,
which He has freely given us in the One He loves."

EPHESIANS 1:3-6, NIV

Once a person is adopted—the adoption cannot be retracted. Once adopted, always adopted!

A couple of years ago, we visited our daughter's family in Northwest Arkansas. We decided to go to a Mexican restaurant in Bentonville because it was one of our grandson Kaleb's favorite establishments. He kept telling me he wanted to show me something.

As we entered the restaurant, he said, Papa, you're not going to believe this new app I have on my phone. Kids know about apps, don't they? I had no idea what I was about to discover.

We got a table for eight and sat down to order our food. Then, Kaleb pulled out his phone and directed it at several cases of Coca-Cola bottles stationed a short distance away. The bottles were written in Spanish.

He messed with the phone until he found the right app and pointed it in the direction of the soft drinks while handing me the phone. He asked me to look at the bottles through the camera on the phone.

When I looked at the bottles through the app, the writing was in English. My head jumped back in disbelief that there was such an app. When I looked at the bottles directly without the phone, they were in Spanish. I put the phone back up to my eyes, and the bottles read in English. I went back and forth, Spanish, then English, and so on.

I knew there was a message in the bottle. I paused, asking God to show me the meaning, and then it hit me like a load of bricks.

It was as if God said, "This is how I see you through the lens of Jesus."

What? Give me more, I thought.

"Now that you know Me as your Father, you are positioned in Christ. When I see Jesus, I see you, perfect, deeply loved, and accepted completely."

Wow! I am positioned in Christ. God sees me through the window of Jesus. What better identity and position is there? None!

An interesting twist is that the back of my phone was a crimson red, reminding me that because of Jesus' shed blood, I'm now viewed differently in Christ by God.

* * *

Only by the work of the Holy Spirit can we have a God encounter where the eyes and ears of our heart are opened to the truth of our identity in Christ.

* * *

When you become a believer, you are in Christ. In His death on the cross, righteousness has been granted to those who believe in Him.[3] This is a positional truth. Immovable—nothing can snatch you from God's hand.[4] When you receive salvation, you become an heir of God—His child—a joint heir with Jesus.[5] This is your identity. You are God's beloved, chosen child. Adopted into the family of God. Your identity and your position are secure.

We do not earn this position; it is freely given to us. With this standing comes the same power and authority that Jesus has over the darkness of this world. We can take these claims in scripture and exercise them in our life to break free from any bondage. Pause right now. Tell the Lord that you are serious about your commitment to understanding your position in Him.

> *Father God, Most Holy One! I ask for Your help to search the scriptures and give light to the eyes and ears of my heart and mind. I pray that I may understand my identity, position, and the power and authority that I have in You. Amen.*

WOUNDS HEALED AND FORGIVENESS GRANTED

When I was young, I had some father wounds that caused me years of anguish because they served as entry points for the enemy. The day I became healed from the wounds was the day forgiveness manifested itself in my relationship with my dad. Forgiveness provides amazing relief from anxiety.

Emotional wounds are entry points for the enemy. If we want to be hassled less by his tactics, we must deal with our wounds and forgive those who violated us. Wounds can come from childhood or adult abuse, divorce, illness, accidents, breakups in relationships, job terminations, premature death of loved ones, and many other things. Anger and fear are usually fruits of these afflictions, and they come at us in many ways with false messages, often causing shame and condemnation. Wounds send us negative messages about ourselves and our faith in God's ability to work for the good.

Wounds can also affect our ability to forgive. Forgiveness is foundational to our faith. Harboring resentment and bitterness eats at our soul—like a drug addiction where our body needs a fix. To ask someone for forgiveness or receive forgiveness from another is a vulnerable action requiring humility to accomplish. Asking for forgiveness requires setting down pride and reaching out to another with a heart to reconcile something lost. Forgiveness is at the core of being a Christian, and God loves it.

If you struggle with forgiveness, start by praying a blessing over those who violated you. Forgive them by faith, even if you don't yet feel like it is real, and ask God to bless them. Not an easy action item. When you can remember the event without reliving it, forgiveness has been achieved; freedom from the wound has been gained.

BREAK FREE FROM STRONGHOLDS

As believers in Jesus Christ, we are in the awesome position to come against any stronghold in our life that sets out to interfere with our emotions and God's plan for us. Under the security of our position in Christ, we have the tools to access God's power to break free from any circumstance that attempts to thwart God's direction. These tools help us be released from our deepest fears, abuses of all kinds, various addictions, and anything else that keeps us from gaining spiritual maturity.

LINKING GOD'S DEEP LOVE TO HURTFUL EXPERIENCES

HEARING WELL?

Hearing something in our head is an indicator to pay attention and listen for the source. We can actually learn a lot if we connect to the source. Is it coming from within or without? As believers, we can listen for the Holy Spirit, and His words have a loving tone to them, even if they bring conviction. Words of condemnation are not from the Holy Spirit. In my journey, most of my hassles have come from within. The enemy may use somebody from the outside to blow a whisper of condemnation in my ear that the flesh partners with but most of my issues have come from within, centered around unresolved wounds.

I believe that the enemy cannot indwell a believer. The Spirit and the enemy cannot occupy the same place or space. So when we hear something condemning, it most likely is the old man repeating old nature, unredeemed themes. Wounds are entry points for the flesh to do battle with the Spirit. Not every wound is an enemy attack. People have free will, and sometimes they hurt us. But regardless of the wound's origin, it requires our attention to get past the hurts and begin healing. Once healing occurs, the hassles that come are only minor incidents needing small tweaking with words that bring life. They are now like a small weed in a well-mulched, well-tended garden—easily plucked out. They are no longer like a giant overgrown bush with sprawling roots that choke out the seeds we have chosen to cultivate.

It is important to locate and understand the source of a wound. Listen well to Holy Spirit! Wounds don't go away easily without some emotional work, which is tough and may take some time. Most likely, the negative voices we hear come from within as the Holy Spirit attempts to take us to a higher level of spiritual maturity.

It is important to locate and understand the source of a wound

As you work out your wounds, they will lose their power. Be careful not to give Satan more credit than he deserves. We can often blame the enemy and not take responsibility for our healing. The devil's power is finite. Limited. He and his minions may be around, but they are helpless against a knowledgeable believer or seasoned warrior in Christ. The Breastplate of Righteousness will protect you from his attack.

PERSEVERANCE

I was in my third year in the major leagues (1976) when it became clear that if I did not improve on my hitting, I would lose my job to someone else soon. One of my veteran teammates began working with me on a new approach. I worked hard to understand how to hit the ball to right field for almost a year before I successfully put it into play during a game. It took a lot of sweat and hard work, but I was willing to put forth the effort because my livelihood depended upon it. The success of my career was a stake, and I needed to connect with what the other player was saying to help me.

Likewise, linking God's deep love to hurtful experiences is not an overnight endeavor. The "putting on" of the Breastplate of Righteousness will take time to master as the Lord transforms your mind to this way of processing your wounds. Access is immediate but grasping and claiming the four basic doctrines in our life—Forgiven, Approved, Deeply Loved, and Made New—takes time.

Being forgiven, approved, deeply loved, and made new are not concepts we can drive up to, order, and have in a few minutes. It will take time, patience, and perseverance as we allow the Lord to reshape and restore our hearts until the work is done. The success of navigating the journey of life will depend on your ability to grasp this deep love that God has for you.

JUSTIFICATION, RECONCILIATION, PROPITIATION, REGENERATION

The basic doctrines of Justification, Reconciliation, Propitiation, and Regeneration are spelled out in the New Testament, where we discover our true identity as Christians. Faithfully studying these principles requires effort to understand clearly what each doctrine means. It is yours to access and the responsibility of every believer to learn to use.

JUSTIFICATION: FAILED OR FORGIVEN?

When I was ten years old, I played baseball in a league for nine to twelve-year-olds. I was one of the younger and smaller players on the team, but I hit three home runs in one particular game and struck out only once in four times to the plate. I sensed from the reaction of others that it was a pretty good accomplishment.

After the game, I asked my dad what he thought of my performance. All I wanted was his approval and acknowledgment of a job well done. My dad responded, "Jim, when you struck out, you would have hit another home run if you had not dropped your elbow. Next time, keep your elbow up."

I had no clue how those words would come back and haunt me with piercing messages in my young adult life. Messages that would translate into, "Jim, you're not doing good enough." "Jim, you have to be perfect." "Jim, you cannot make any mistakes." My dad meant well, and I have known for some time now that he loves me deeply and was doing what he thought a good parent should do. My dad passed away in January of '21, and I am pleased to say we were in a good spot with our relationship. The wound was not intentional or malicious, but the blow to my identity was real and had lasting effects.

I found myself a few years along in the start of a great career, but I was miserable and did not like myself. No matter how well I did, I saw myself as a failure every time I turned around. I could not get those messages out of my head, and it was killing me emotionally. If I got one hit, I should have gotten two. If I got two hits, I should have gotten three, and so on. I was never satisfied; always frustrated with my performance.

I became a Christian in 1977, but the performance trap continued to haunt me for several more years before God gradually replaced those messages with new ones. The entire healing process took almost fifteen years, but it took only a few years before I began to feel some consistent relief.

WHAT IS JUSTIFICATION?

Justification means that we have a loving God who forgives us of our sins and has granted us the righteousness of Christ. Because of justification, I share in Christ's righteousness and am, therefore, **fully pleasing to the father.**[6] Read that again—fully pleasing to the Father! Can this be true? How does that feel? Oh God, I need to know how this feels! Please let me know what it is like to be pleasing to You!

Though it took time, little by little, I began to connect with this passage in Romans 5. As I spent time with the Lord, He quickened my mind and opened my heart to its meaning. Only through the work of the Holy Spirit can understanding be gained. Once this paradigm shift occurs, you are changed forever.

HOW CAN I APPLY THIS TRUTH?

I apply this truth by linking God's deep love to my hurtful experiences.

Once you connect to the meaning of a passage, you see it in a new way. You can apply this shift in your thinking to a past hurt and experience its healing power. Let me show you how another person taught me. The following is a visual of the process that led me to break free from the fear of failure.

EXPERIENCE
10 years old: 3 home runs and 1 strikeout at a ballgame.

FALSE MESSAGE
"You're not doing good enough."

INITIAL INTERPRETATION
Failure.

NEW MESSAGE
"I now see you through the eyes of Jesus."
"You are perfect in my sight."
"I love you deeply."

A hurtful experience delivered a false message (lie). I interpreted the message in a way that harmed my identity. Once identified, I replaced the lie with the truth (new message). Forgiveness was established, and healing began.

RECONCILIATION: REJECTED OR APPROVED?

As I look back at my early childhood, it seems that I had the tendency to want the approval of others. I desired to please others, or more truthfully, I desired to please my father. Going back to my pre-school years, I always seemed to enjoy performing for applause. I liked a good response to something I would say or do.

I recall many conversations with my father about what "so and so thought about my performance. Whether dad had heard a good statement or a bad one, it seemed to be very important to him what other people were saying about his son. I naturally picked up on this very early in my life, and by the time I was a young adult, the roots of an approval addict were deeply entrenched. When I was in the ninth grade, an incident fueled these emotions for approval.

I was one of the starting half-backs on our football team. Football was really not my thing, but there I was anyway. The season was coming to a close, and we were preparing to play the cross-town rival for the city championship. We had been practicing on a play for two weeks that previously had not been used. It was a passing play designed for me to run straight ahead through the line and downfield where it was to leave me wide open for the pass and, therefore, the game victory. Our coach had been keeping it as a secret weapon to be brought out and used at the appropriate time.

We were late in the fourth quarter and down by six points when the special play came to the huddle. The ball was hiked, I ran my pattern, and sure enough, the play left me wide open on our five-yard line for the pass. I looked up as the ball came to me, but I dropped it. I was standing down there in the end zone all by myself with the football lying on the ground and everybody looking on. I mean everybody—including those who give my dad feedback on my performance.

In sports, words aren't needed to get feedback. I have been around the sports culture my whole life. When you lose or fail, there is an eerie quietness that can be cut with a knife. The silence might be a courtesy from some, but for a young athlete, it can be received as rejection. At least, that is the way I felt it, and the feeling was horrible.

WHAT IS RECONCILIATION?

Reconciliation is the main theme behind Jesus' death on the cross. **Reconciliation means that while I was once unreceptive toward God and separated from Him, I am now forgiven and have been brought into an intimate relationship with Him.** Through the spilled blood of Christ, man has been brought into union with God. Therefore, **I am totally accepted by God.**

God forgives you of your shortcomings and accepts you without conditions. You don't need the approval of others to feel good about yourself. God's acceptance is based on His goodness, not yours. You are completely, totally accepted by your Father!

Learning this was incredible, but it took time for the healing power of God to work in me. Later, God gave me a phrase that shields my heart (like a breastplate)! It goes like this, "Rejection is God's Re-direction!"

When you can take a different angle on a hurtful event, it is a powerful tool to pick yourself up and continue on. Through the work of the Holy Spirit in your mind and heart, you are changed forever. I can say today with great satisfaction that rejection no longer has the power it once had in my life.

HOW CAN I APPLY THIS TRUTH?

The following shows the process of how the Lord led me to break free from the fear of rejection.

EXPERIENCE
Ninth grade football game: dropped a pass.

FALSE MESSAGE
"My acceptance depends on my performance."

INITIAL INTERPRETATION
Rejection.

NEW MESSAGE
"I am totally accepted and loved just as I am."

Recall that wounds are easy access points for your soul's enemy. At the end of this chapter, you will be given the opportunity to begin the process of breaking free from any strongholds that may exist in your life. It will take the support of others for this process to be successful.

PROPITIATION: BLAMED OR DEEPLY LOVED?

When I was around eight years old, I was working on my bike outside the house. I loved being outside. I grew up living across the street from a baseball park, and I could not wait until the morning to wake up and head to the park to play. This particular morning though, I was close to the house and trying to fix the chain on my bike. With the wrench in my hand, I was trying to loosen a bolt when my hand slipped, causing my thumb great pain. Reacting, I cried out, "Sunny beach!" You know, like a sunny day at the beach and not the son of the female dog (if you know what I mean).

I did not realize that my father was hidden a few feet away, working in the garage. My dad had this thing against cussing. Years later, I learned the root of this was associated with his grandfather, who could cuss up a storm. This embarrassed my dad, so he was determined that none of his children would use foul language.

My dad peeled around the corner of the garage, growling, "What did I hear you say?"

"You know, dad?" I said, "… like a sunny day at the beach …" sheepishly, I tried to explain my position.

My dad lifted me off the ground, hauling me in the air through every door on the way back to my bedroom, where the real discipline started. He shook me until my head and neck began to hurt—a lot. I sobbed as I looked into the angry eyes of someone who appeared not to like me. That

76

look of wrath would trouble me for years. This incident had a traumatic effect on me in many ways. I became afraid of punishment and began to blame others for personal failure. Gradually, I withdrew from others and even from God.

As I lay there sobbing and looking into the livid eyes of my father, not understanding what had caused such intense anger. I asked him, "What was it that I did so wrong?"

He answered, "It's not what you <u>said</u> but what you were <u>thinking</u> that was wrong!"

Now an eight-year-old does not know how to process those intense emotions or analyze their possible effect. As an adult, I would realize, as I looked back, that I felt unloved by my dad. I believed his love was based on my performance and that if I ever fell short of the standard set before me, I might have to endure punishment. I had trouble dealing with authority figures along the way. The wrath, deep rejection, and intense scolding for what I was thinking led me into emotional isolation. This incident was so profound because failure, rejection, blame, and shame were all connected to this single event. As an adult, I entered a high-profile, highly stressful career in professional sports, and this unresolved childhood wound drove me to avoidance.

WHAT IS PROPITIATION?

Propitiation delivers the warm, soothing message to our soul: Christ's death on the cross satisfied God's wrath toward man; therefore, I am deeply loved by God.[7] What a wonderful thought—to know that as a believer in Christ, we no longer come under the wrath of God. We have moved from a position of wrath to being under the umbrella of God's grace. His discipline is a loving response that hems us in, not a punitive response. This place of love puts us in a situation where God's discipline takes on a much different look—one of gentle adjustment for our good rather than that of one who drops the hammer on us in anger.

I needed to connect with the freedom I have in a personal relationship with Christ. I needed to have the flexibility to make mistakes in my life (grace) and not feel condemned. Through God's Word and the work of the Holy Spirit, my relationship with Christ was the answer to filling the deep void and removing the restlessness that had so long existed.

Periodically, I would still have to confront these elements that tried to interfere with my emotional balance, but they would never again have the power over me that they once had.

HOW CAN I APPLY THIS TRUTH?

The following shows the process of how the Lord led me to break free from the blame game.

EXPERIENCE
8 years old: Bicycle/Hurt Thumb/"Sunny Beach!"

FALSE MESSAGE
"There is something wrong with the way you think."

INITIAL INTERPRETATION
Blame.

NEW MESSAGE
"You didn't do anything wrong."
"You are creative."

REGENERATED: SHAMED OR MADE NEW?

This next incident is probably the most difficult for me to share because it involved sexual abuse by an older neighbor boy. I wanted to shovel it under the doormat. It was embarrassing and shameful to be involved in such an evil act imposed by another!

I was advanced beyond my years in playing baseball, so the older boys in the neighborhood often invited me to play with them. After one of the morning games, a boy about four years older, who I trusted at the time, asked me if I wanted to play a game in the dug-out. I loved playing games but not the kind where I found my pants down and someone fondling me. I pulled away very quickly and started to cry as I ran for home.

The way to handle such things back then was to ignore them, and maybe they would go away. He never tried it again, but it left a bunch of feelings churning inside that would not have the chance to come out for years. The shame from this incident stayed locked up inside, resulting in me pulling away from others, especially men. I was almost thirty before I was comfortable in a close relationship with a male—including getting close to a loving God in my early years as a Christian.

WHAT IS REGENERATION?

Regeneration means that I am complete, a new creation in Christ; the old person I used to be is gone, and a new one has come.[8] The world tells us that an indicator of the future can be determined by looking at the pattern of the past. This does not have to be true in the life of a believer. God's Spirit transforms us—we are made new.

We can be assured that as believers in Christ, we do not have to be held in bondage to something in our past. Feelings of shame over the sexual abuse of another (or any sin in general) do not have to keep us from relationships or from approaching a loving and Holy God.

HOW CAN I APPLY THIS TRUTH?

The following shows how the Lord led me to process shame in my life.

EXPERIENCE
8 years old: Sexual abuse.

FALSE MESSAGE
"Let's not talk about this."
"Some things are better kept a secret."

INITIAL INTERPRETATION
Shame.

NEW MESSAGE
"I am glad you came to me to share your deepest feelings."
"You are complete; you are safe and loved."

Freedom begins with learning the truth. The truth sets you free. But the longer you have been a prisoner to lies, the longer it can take to live as a free man. Breaking free often requires a process to renew your mind, break behavior loops, and think differently. Your journey to freedom will not be done alone or hidden in a closet.

FOUR COMMON ENTRY POINTS

I have given you four of the most common methods the dark forces in the spiritual realm will use to come after us (failure, rejection, blame, shame). Others that spin off these include anger, neglect, abandonment, and more. The enemy has numerous ways to deceive, confuse, and distort the truth, but the issues of failure, rejection, blame, and shame are the most common themes used in the spiritual battle against us.

Another way to look at these four doctrines put together into one statement is this:

"We are cherished children of God, selected for this time in all of eternity, deeply loved, accepted, and approved by Him for a wonderful purpose."

Grasp these concepts, and you have put on the Breastplate of Righteousness.

GOD'S LOVE: EARTHLY DAD—HEAVENLY DADDY

PERFECT PARENT

If you have gotten the impression that I had some hard feelings toward my dad, you are right. However, there are times that my dad is my hero once again, as he was when I was a young boy. As this trip comes full circle, it indicates that my healing process has come to a close.

My dad had good intentions. He did with his children what most parents try to do with their kids—the best job we can with whatever information we have. No matter how skilled or informed a parent may be in modeling God's love; we are all fallen beings who come short of the mark.[9] Even for the best of us, there will be incidents when we fail to love or support our children in a way that only a Holy God can.

I am now thankful that my earthly dad was not perfect because I have come to know and experience an awesome and loving relationship with a perfect heavenly Father through my dad's imperfections. Today, I wouldn't have wanted it any other way!

---••• •---

Gratitude is another indication that healing has happened.

---••• •---

Abba Father simply means "Daddy!" We all try to be good parents, but there is only one perfect parent in our Heavenly Daddy—where a close, loving, and intimate relationship with true significance is found.

FINDING SIGNIFICANCE

In Roman times, the breastplate that protected the soldier's vital organs also communicated their rank. Rank showed a position of authority and power conveyed by unspoken words of pride. We still see this in the military uniforms of today. Officers wear their uniform with stars, stripes, and medals of bravery emblazoned across the front or sides of their apparel. As consumers, we try to convey the same sense of significance from our clothing through the use of designer wear and their logos. The concept of finding pride through a symbol is throughout our society.

Growing up in Galesburg, Illinois, I received the message loud and clear, "Jim, if you become a Major League baseball player, you will have everything that life has to offer—fame, fortune, power, and luxury."

I was in the fourth year of my baseball career (1977) when I came to the stark realization that those earlier messages were not true. I was at a juncture where success at the highest level was being experienced, yet the sense of having significance in my life was void. I began to search, only to find that I would be driven back to the idea that unless Jesus Christ were in my life, I would not have true happiness or find a deep sense of significance.

I stumbled along in my early years as a Christian, not really getting it. In fact, my first few years as a believer seemed to be more difficult than the years before I got saved. Much of that had to do with not understanding the Bible and not reading it consistently. It was not until God led me into discovering the concepts of justification, reconciliation, propitiation, and regeneration that I began to experience true significance. I also found another benefit: the things that I had acquired, which I thought would bring me joy in the first place and didn't, I began to enjoy in a different, more exciting way.

Over the years, I have watched as very successful men and women jump from one endeavor to another in the hopes that on the next deal or next toy, they will find that deep sense of satisfaction that lasts. It will never happen! It also occurs on the other side of the economic ladder. People with very little money think that if they just had more of it, they would be all right. Statements like, "If only I could win the lottery," or "If only I could catch a break," or "If only I could get this to fall in place …" King Solomon said it this way:

> "Two things I ask of you, O Lord;
> Do not refuse me before I die:
> Keep falsehood and lies far from me;
> Give me neither poverty or riches,
> But give me only my daily bread.
> Otherwise, I may have too much and
> disown You and say, 'Who is the Lord?'
> Or that I may become poor and steal,
> And so dishonor the name of my God."
>
> PROVERBS 30:7-9, NIV

Solomon's heart was in the right spot, and as a result, God gave him unbelievable riches. But Solomon was right! I've observed those who shun God on both sides of the economic ladder—those so wealthy there is no time or need for God, those so poor they believe God has abandoned them. Both groups have decided to go it alone, seeking significance outside of God.

A true sense of significance only comes in a personal relationship with God through Jesus. The starting point for finding significance is to receive Him as Lord and Savior. Putting on our spiritual armor and learning how to wage spiritual warfare will take time. Soldiers are not battle-ready on day one of basic training.

Several years ago, I spoke to a youth group at a church in Ft. Worth. After the message, the youth pastor invited me into the back classroom to show me something of great importance. When I entered the room, there was a life-size cross on the opposite side of the room. As I approached the cross, two ropes were tied in knots, each on both ends of the upper part. The youth pastor asked me if I wanted to put my hands through the ropes and hang on the wooden structure. I hesitated a bit, with several negative thoughts swirling through my head. After a couple of minutes of looking at the cross, I decided I would give it a try.

There are people I love dearly in this world—my wife, kids, grandkids, and friends but my first reaction upon hanging was, "I couldn't die for anyone!" There was a terrible feeling of anxiety about being trapped; my elbows and shoulders were killing me. I had no leverage to pull myself into a position of strength. I had trouble breathing. It was an awful experience. I yelled at the youth pastor to help me down after just 10 seconds of hanging.

This experience brought a fresh connection for me to what Jesus went through while also knowing in advance what He was about to do. Before the cross, He sweat blood in the garden. This blood flow from His face showed extreme stress.[10] Even so, He went to the cross out of love and obedience to the Father. He went so we could be reconciled to God.

"For God so loved the world that He gave His
one and only Son, that whoever believes in Him
shall not perish but have eternal life."

JOHN 3:16, NIV

Jesus died an awful death on the cross because of His deep love for us. There is no greater love than when one lays down his life for another and no greater place of significance than His act of love.[11]

ENEMY'S TACTIC

ATTACKING GOD'S LOVE

When we look at the first five verses of Genesis 3, we can read the dialogue between the serpent and Eve. "For God knows that when you eat from the fruit of the trees, your eyes will be open, and you will be like God, knowing good and evil."[12]

If we look behind that statement, we see the serpent suggests that God doesn't really care for their best. "God really doesn't love you." He taunts, "Stick with me, and I'll care for you better than He will." Satan deceived Eve into thinking that God was withholding something of great value, so she rebelled against God and took Adam along with her.

Regarding the Breastplate of Righteousness, the enemy's tactics center around the idea of twisting God's deep love for us, attempting to disrupt our significance and our ability to receive God's love. He will try to convince us that the work of Christ on the cross is not sufficient for us to be fully pleasing, totally accepted, deeply loved, and complete in Christ. It is our responsibility as believers to recognize the devil's schemes and then deliver the knockout blow by exercising the Word of God.

As a parent and now as a grandparent, I can tell you that my love is so deep for my kids that I will not withhold anything of great value.

If I do not have it in my possession, I will make adjustments to find it and deliver it. Whether it is a demonstration of love, a material object, a spiritual lesson, or an emotional encouragement, I will try to do whatever it will take to provide for the need. The Lord is so much a better parent than I can ever think about being.

His love is perfect.

SUMMARY

FOUNDATIONAL FOR INTERNAL FREEDOM AND SPIRITUAL MATURITY

The Breastplate of Righteousness comes right after the Belt of Truth. The two form the foundational elements for internal freedom and spiritual maturity that better equips us for spiritual warfare. Truth applied to the fractured crevices in our heart becomes the place by which we can break free from any strongholds.

When the truth of God's Word (the four principles we just studied) are linked to our past hurts, an incredible release of our true potential sets the stage for us to become spiritually mature. We can take this inner transformation by the Holy Spirit and use it to participate with God in advancing His Kingdom (where our feet become fitted with the readiness that comes from the Gospel of Peace). A person who successfully navigates this path will experience a newness that demonstrates peace in the relationships around them. This new sense of purpose in Christ releases us to join the Lord in His work.

STEP UP TO THE PLATE

As you find a place to be alone and quiet for this exercise, listen to these two songs and let their words soak into your heart.

- "Good Good Father" by Chris Tomlin.

- "Unstoppable Love" by Kim Walker-Smith and Jesus Culture.

1. In your own words, what does **JUSTIFICATION** now mean to you?

2. In your own words, what does **RECONCILIATION** now mean to you?

3. In your own words, what does **PROPITIATION** now mean to you?

4. In your own words, what does **REGENERATION** now mean to you?

5. Wounds are entry points for the enemy. From your understanding of the four common entry points (failure, rejection, blame, and shame), which one are you more prone to?

    Why? How would Jesus respond to this?

6. Try this Breaking Free exercise. (Repeat this exercise as many times as you need to work through issues affecting your identity and position in Christ.)

    EXPERIENCE
    Identify a painful experience.

    FALSE MESSAGE
    Think about the false message you received due to this emotional wound.

    INITIAL INTERPRETATION
    What was your initial interpretation (failure, rejection, blame, or shame)?

    NEW MESSAGE
    Then spend time with the Holy Spirit to help you unpack the incident and let Him link His deep love to this hurtful experience.

ENDNOTES

1. See Ephesians 3:17-19.
2. See Ephesians 1:7-10.
3. 2 Corinthians 5:21.
4. John 10:28-30.
5. Romans 8:17.
6. Romans 5:1.
7. 1 John 4:9-11.
8. 2 Corinthians 5:17.
9. Romans 3:23.
10. Luke 22:44.
11. John 15:13.
12. Genesis 3:5, NIV.

———— • • • ————

*Putting on our spiritual armor
and learning how to wage
spiritual warfare will take time.
Soldiers are not battle-ready
on day one of basic training.*

———— • • • ————

Kingdom Building

READY SHOES—FEET FITTED WITH THE
READINESS OF THE GOSPEL OF PEACE

SHIELD OF FAITH

When we connect with Jesus and receive the truth of His Word, we are freed to experience the power of God working through us. As we become equipped—wearing the full armor of God and skilled in spiritual warfare—He uses us to build His Kingdom of believers.

Successfully applying the **Belt of Truth** and the **Breastplate of Righteousness** results in an inner transformation by the Holy Spirit. We experience internal peace as love flows from within to those around us. We become vulnerable as we realize we are safe—the Breastplate protects our heart. We can now be genuine as our emotional state is re-born, and religious forms are done away with. Our healing forms the message we share with the world. This becomes the word of our testimony that we use to influence the world for Christ. We are growing powerful and effective in ministry.

The bolder we become in sharing Christ, the more alert we need to be as we enter a new level of warfare. We must rely more deeply on our relationship with God for survival. As we do, we grow in power and an even deeper commitment to pursue God. This type of living makes it hard for anyone or anything to capsize us. Our trust in Christ is established, and we can endure or sustain any situation.

As we move to the next two armor pieces, the title "Kingdom Building" emerged as a central theme for this section. We lace up our **Ready Shoes**—our feet are fitted with the readiness of the Gospel of Peace, and we pick up the **Shield of Faith**. These armor pieces refer to a stance or posture of advancing God's Kingdom through our testimony and acts of faith.

Chapter Three

READY SHOES

FEET FITTED WITH THE READINESS
THAT COMES FROM THE
GOSPEL OF PEACE

WHAT DO READY SHOES MEAN?

When our feet are fitted with the readiness that comes from the Gospel of Peace, we are able to stand our ground—have solid footing—with God.

WHY ARE THEY IMPORTANT?

The Ready Shoes relate to our ability to experience God and share the Good News about Him with others. When we wear them, we unleash the power of our testimony.

HOW DO I "PUT ON" THE READY SHOES?

I put on the Ready Shoes when I become grounded in the Word of God, standing on a firm foundation, I am in a state of readiness to join God in carrying out the Great Commission as I walk out my faith authentically.

WHAT IS A TWO-WORD RESULT I CAN EXPECT
FOR APPLYING THE READY SHOES?

Always Armed

WHAT ARE THE ENEMY'S TACTICS?

The enemy seeks to destroy our testimony and make us ashamed to share the Gospel.

WHAT ROLE DOES APPLYING THE READY SHOES PLAY IN SPIRITUAL MATURITY?

- *Keeps me in a state of readiness—always prepared for ministry and always armed for spiritual warfare*

- *Unleashes the power of my testimony— prepares me for the Great Commission*

- *Provide me with firm footing—I am not easily swayed by false doctrines or ideologies*

SHOES: PREPARED AND READY

DUAL USAGE

A baseball player wears a couple of different types of shoes, so he is ready for whatever turf he is playing on. A particular shoe will grip the turf, giving him readiness, stability, and tactical movement. A steal-cleated shoe is generally worn on natural grass surfaces to grip both the grass surface and the dirt portion. A rubberized multi-surface shoe is worn on artificial turf fields.

A Roman soldier wore a cleated shoe called a caligae that would give him balance, stability, and tactical mobility to stand his ground. The worst thing that could happen to a soldier was losing his balance and falling to the ground, rendering him almost ineffective. The weight of the armor made it difficult to get back to his feet.

So we see in both the baseball player and the Roman soldier the need to be fitted with a shoe that gives readiness, stability, and balance to navigate their turf effectively and stand their ground. In the spiritual realm, we stand our ground by being ready to move with our testimony to others or ready to fight the enemy. This armor piece serves a dual purpose.

STANDING YOUR GROUND WITH GOD—A STATE OF READINESS

COST OF FREEDOM

Though the Ready Shoes have multiple purposes, all lead back to one concept—walking with God. When you receive the truth about God's deep love for you and apply those truths to your hurtful experiences and receive healing, it results in three tightly connected things.

- An inner transformation that brings peace (freedom),

- a natural outflow of love (testimony),

- the resulting readiness to join God (availability).

This makes for a powerful and genuine expression of God's love for the world around us through our life.

I was recently listening to a talk radio program, where a man was communicating about the price of freedom. This gentleman gave testimony of the number of times he had been to a veteran's hospital to visit his dad in recovery. Upon his numerous trips to the hospital, he reflected on a sign that hung there saying, "The price of freedom is visible here." It made me realize that anything of great value comes with a price. Many have given their lives and have had their bodies ravaged during wars so that future generations could experience the great freedoms that Americans have had over the years.

Behind any eventual inner transformation of a believer is a price that has been paid. First is the price that Jesus paid with His blood on the cross at Calvary, which set the stage for our inner transformation. Second is the brave and courageous journey we pursue for our healing as we apply the truths of what the cross represents to bring about that transformation. Any major healing process, whether physical or emotional, is difficult.

In Old Testament times, Israelite men were circumcised as a symbolic gesture of their covenant relationship with God. It was an act where a man had a piece of the most private area of his body cut in order to represent his belief in God. In the New Testament, though, we see a circumcision of the heart where God cuts or reshapes it as a heart towards Him.

This process of reshaping hearts can be painful, which is the price we pay for spiritual maturity. This can be viewed as symbolic of the new life in Christ. For some, the pain can be so intense that by the time they come out on the other end, it is as if they have experienced emotional death and were then resurrected by God. Those who have experienced such an intense process emerge with a deeper understanding of the resurrection of Christ. Their testimony is powerful in connecting others to the power of Christ.

I have heard it said that "whatever doesn't kill you makes you stronger." Those who endure come through with either a grateful, humble resolve to pursue God forever or a streak of pride in their accomplishment that will trip them up in the future.

True inner transformation results in peace. In some cases, the level of peace in a believer's life can be associated to the amount of pain they have experienced. They have paid the price, and the result of the price paid for inner freedom is peace

THE POWER OF YOUR TESTIMONY

I have listened to many people speak over the years. It always amazes men when someone with very little experience in public speaking gives a powerful message. Invariably, it happens when someone shares a personal life-changing event. It doesn't matter if their delivery is polished or professional—they captivate you with their testimony, and they are a joy to hear!

The most exciting stories are those in which God has done a work in a person's life. Those stories reach right down to the core and bring life to all who hear them. When you have been transformed, it is hard to contain the excitement of what God has done. There is nothing fake about it, no posing on the speaker's part. There is a natural outpouring of God's goodness, not only in their testimony but in their walk, that is contagious.

In chapter one, I talked about standing on the mound with manager Dick Howser in 1986, a year after the Royals won the World Series. Dick had just removed David Cone, one of our bright young pitchers. I looked at Dick and said, "You look tired. Are you feeling okay?"

Dick responded, "No, as a matter of fact, I do not feel well at all!"

A few days later, Dick collapsed and was taken to the hospital. It was determined that he had an aggressive brain tumor.

My relationship with Dick had always been professional. We did not really have any time alone to get to know each other outside of baseball, but there was always mutual respect. He was the best manager I had ever played under, and that is saying something since I ended up playing for fourteen managers in sixteen years.

Several days after his first surgery, Dick called me to set up a meeting. I wasn't sure what it was about, and when I arrived a few days later, I was caught off guard by his comment to me. "Jim, I have noticed something different about you over the last year, and I want to know more about it. You show real consistency in the way you carry yourself. What is it?"

I had never had this opportunity present itself to me in such a way. I had heard others share these stories, but it had not happened to me before. I was aware scripture instructed me to be ready to share the light that shines in my life when asked, and this would be one of the most special moments in my life. I shared with Dick how Christ had become the center of my life and had changed my heart. What an experience it was for me!

I do not know if Dick accepted Christ that day, but I do know he soon began sharing his testimony with others. He would never again manage a regular-season game after that day we spent on the mound together, and before a year was up, Dick joined the Lord in Paradise.

Looking back, I can't take credit for anything other than showing up and being ready. Dick saw a glimpse of God in me that attracted him. I didn't think at the time anyone noticed my walk, but somehow he got a glance of Jesus through my life. What a joy to be able to join God in His work. There was no pressure to perform. No one's salvation is up to me; only God can do that work. The burden of salvation is not on my shoulders; all I have to do is show up and be ready to share my testimony.

God prompts us to join Him, then we act. Instead of launching out on our own, through a window of performance and getting into enemy territory without God at our side, we move in sensitivity to the Holy Spirit, walking with God, joining Him in His plan and in His power. Our feet become fitted with the readiness of the Gospel of Peace as we prepare ourselves with our testimony. We use it as a witness to share Christ with others, or we use it in warfare, reminding us and our enemy that we have overcome by the blood of the Lamb.

God prompts us to join Him, then we act

When we put on the Breastplate of Righteousness, we learned the importance of forgiveness and reconciliation. Under the surface, unresolved conflict fuels the flames of anger—anger that transfers our power to another. We taste freedom as we gain back the power we lost by confronting and resolving conflict, and we become a better conduit for allowing God to transfer His power through us. The words of our testimony flow from God through us and quicken life in those who hear.

I grew up religiously going to church every Sunday, but it wasn't until I was twenty-six that I received Christ into my life. The distinct difference between where I was then and where I am now is the realization that Christianity is a relationship with Christ, rooted in grace and love, and not a set of ritualistic acts based on performance. Acts of performance can be characterized as asking God to join us in our work to meet our goals. There is no power from God behind this approach, and performing legalistic acts of service quickly burns you out.

Genuine Christianity asks, "Lord, how can I join You in Your work today?" This question demonstrates inner peace and comfort in trusting God to control the process of advancing His Kingdom. Wearing the Ready Shoes makes us available and sensitive to His calling and then joining Him. This leads to experiencing God through powerful and effective ministry.

ALWAYS ARMED

STATE OF READINESS

What a blessing and a release of pressure to realize that all I have to do at times is show up and be available for God. In his book, *Experiencing God*, Henry Blackaby says, "Find out where God is working and join Him." I got this thing about "evangelism" all wrong for years. I cannot tell you how many times, having good intentions, I got my nose bloodied by rejection by trying to force square words into unreceptive holes—maybe even more accurate, throwing my pearls before swine.

Who am I to tell God to join me in His work so that I can put another notch on my belt for recognition? As a believer, do I always need to find some means of justifying my spiritual existence? No. The key to putting on this piece of armor is "being ready" or "always armed" to share the light in our life with others when asked. The other side of readiness is being prepared to respond to any outside forces of evil that may come against me.

Early in my baseball career, I found out that one fundamental to properly blocking balls was anticipating a badly thrown ball in the dirt.

Some pitchers like Hall of Famers Ferguson Jenkins, Gaylord Perry, Don Sutton, and pitcher Bret Saberhagen seldom made errant throws. There were many more pitchers, though, that kept me on my toes with throws that could go anywhere.

After a while, I realized I had more trouble blocking the balls thrown in the dirt by the first group of control specialists because I didn't expect them to be errant. It doesn't take much to be caught off guard and not prepared. With just a little discipline, we can greatly reduce the potential of not being ready. This state of readiness is exactly what it infers—always armed.

Readiness keeps us in a state of resolve, and resolve leads to discipline, and discipline leads to success. I became more disciplined at learning when to be on my toes—which pitchers threw what pitches. In other words, I realized that the wild pitches came on certain pitches, sometimes different for each pitcher.

In the spiritual sense, we can become disciplined at knowing when the conditions are right to share our testimony. For spiritual warfare, we can be alert and on our guard, prepared for whatever wild pitch the enemy throws at us.

PATIENTLY ALERT

I asked my friend, Zig Ziglar, the late motivational speaker, what his favorite book was outside of the Bible. His response surprised me. "*The American Dictionary of the English Language, Noah Webster, 1828,*" he said. Over the years, I have learned to appreciate this as a household item. The 1828 version is a Christian dictionary that includes biblical terms at a time when this was still allowed. So, with my love for the meaning of words in mind, I want to explain the words "patiently alert" separately and then put them together.

Webster's 1828 defines patience as "the suffering of afflictions, pain, toil, calamity, provocation or other evil, **with a calm, unruffled temper; endurance without murmuring or fretfulness**" (emphasis added). Doesn't the first part of the definition sound like stuff you may have to deal with in navigating through the elements of the Breastplate? And doesn't the bold part sound like a person who has successfully applied the Breastplate and come out of those experiences with an internal peace of mind about life?

The second definition of patience is "having the quality of enduring evils without murmuring or fretfulness; sustaining afflictions of body and mind with fortitude, calmness or Christian submission to the divine will." We see a repeated theme of enduring evils without complaint in this definition. In addition, Webster refers to pursuing and waiting (submission) on God in this process of enduring difficulties. Ultimately, our relationship with the divine creator through trials creates patience in our spirit, resulting in internal peace. This peace can only come from an intimate relationship with God and the study of the Gospel of Peace (His Word).

Webster's Dictionary defines alert as "watchful; vigilance; guarding against surprise or danger." It would do us good in our spiritual lives if we developed the same discipline of watchfulness that we see in our military people during combat. I can't imagine seeing Special Forces commandos naively strolling through the mountains of Afghanistan, looking for Osama Bin Laden.

By acquiring this discipline of watchfulness, we will seldom be caught by surprise when God calls us to join Him in the life of another. Likewise, we will not fall into dangerous territory with the enemy who attempts to sneak into our lives under stealth.

When we move to put these two words together, "patiently alert" (always armed), we see a soldier in Christ, whose internal peace and watchful eye keep him showing up prepared to join God in His work to build His Kingdom, allowing God to carry the burden of the outcome. This piece of armor is a natural outflow of God's power through the inner transformation of the Holy Spirit (our testimony), both for effective ministry and to fight the good fight.

The fit of our "Ready Shoes" is conditional on the Gospel of Peace. It is difficult to submit to and join God (in readiness) in His work without it. It is work that we have the awesome privilege to be a part of, and the great relief that we are not responsible for making happen. This attitude of humility should always go before us.

READINESS FOR MINISTRY

AVAILABILITY

If you are a believer in Christ, you are in ministry. The Great Commission is for us all, and we must remain open to opportunities to share the love and light of Christ. We must not become too busy to take cues from the Lord. As we move about our day, we must remain in a state of readiness for the Kingdom.

The Great Commission is for every believer in Christ

In the first book of Kings, the Lord tells Elijah to go to the mountains to "be in the presence of the Lord, for the Lord is about to pass by."[1] Some may contend that this passage is a symbolic indictment against Israel for God to bring judgment on His people. Can we also look at it as a series of possible conditions that begin to portray when God might come to meet with Elijah for Elijah to hear from the Lord? I think we can make a case to do so.

First, a "great and powerful wind" tore the mountains apart and shattered the rocks, but the Lord was not in the wind. Second, there was a "great earthquake," but the Lord was not in the earthquake. After the earthquake came a "fire," but the Lord was not there either. Lastly, after the fire came a "gentle whisper," and it was then that Elijah went out to join the Lord.[2]

God was not in the wind, the earthquake, or the fire. In the same way, He is not in the "busyness" and "whirlwind" of our lifestyle. He is not in the noise or distractions. He is in the secret place. In this exchange between Elijah and the Lord, we see the idea that we must slow down, get away from the distractions, and get quiet before we have a chance to hear from God. That is not to say we can't respond to Him amid distractions. We can. He can speak whenever and wherever He wants. In distraction and distress, He speaks to get us out of harm's way. But generally, to set the stage to receive from Him, it is important to get quiet with Him in the morning consistently. I find my ability to receive from Him enhanced when I start my day this way.

For Christians today, busyness is probably the number one reason for not being sensitive to the Spirit when prompted to take action. This restricts our ability to receive from the Holy Spirit when ministry moments present themselves.

Availability requires us to take moments in our day to rest and slow down so we will be available to join the Lord in His work.

FISHERS OF MEN

I am reminded of a concept that one of my pastors gave me years ago on how to be fishers of men. When we go fishing, several critical pieces of information are important to be a good fisherman. He ran through this formula, which those of you who do fish will not be surprised. Depending on the lake where you fish, the time of year, the water temperature, the time of day, the depth you fish, and the kind of fish you are trying to catch determine what bait you use. When you think about it, this formula takes a healthy understanding of the fish into serious consideration.

In the spiritual sense, when we reach out to others, the same kind of respect and consideration should be taken. Let's look at some of the ways we can be ready to join God. This will free you up and give you a sense of peace about your role in being available for God's work. Later in this section, I will help you connect the element of readiness to spiritual attack and help you connect how unresolved areas of your life and tiredness will negatively affect your ability to do ministry and battle effectively against the enemy.

EYES TO SEE AND EARS TO HEAR

I try to be seeker-friendly as I move about the day with friends and family, in the workplace, in the community, or wherever my day takes me. To me, this makes the most sense. I observe people who need a relationship with God, and when I develop a relationship with them and earn their respect, they are more likely to listen to what I have to say. Out "in the wild" is where we can look to see where people are hurting. Sometimes this is hard to observe in the church, where many are posing and trying to hide their hurts. We must approach the day by asking God to give us "eyes to see and ears to hear."

A couple of years ago, Janet and I were on a trip to Colorado, and we had hauled our bike on the trip so we could observe the mountain's majestic views once we arrived. It was exhilarating to ride as Janet always sat behind me. We decided to leave Vail on one particular day and ride to Steamboat Springs for lunch. It was a great trip with some of the most beautiful scenery. Nothing out of the ordinary had happened, but that was about to change.

As we drew closer to Steamboat, I began to get uncomfortable in my spirit, thinking something bad might happen. It caused me to be more cautious as we made our way to lunch. I noticed that some clouds were developing to the south and moving our way. I wondered if God was trying to warn us about the weather.

We made it to Steamboat and had a great lunch at a restaurant along a creek. We met some fine people and had some interaction, but the thought of danger didn't dissipate. We finished lunch and began our trip back to Vail, about 200 miles away.

Upon leaving the restaurant, I again observed the clouds building and decided to take a different route back that might keep us away from the weather pattern. So we started up the mountain just south of town to escape any potential harm. The new direction didn't deter my sense of danger.

As we reached the top of the mountain onto a level area, I noticed a truck driving erratically behind us. The driver was swerving into the other lane, back and forth he went for a short time. I thought he might be drunk or on drugs, so my attention hit a high pitch. I kept looking in the rearview mirror, wondering if I should pull over and stop, but there was no room to make this move.

All of a sudden, he sped up very close behind us. We could hear the engine in his truck. I thought he would make contact, but he stopped and then pulled back. I continued to watch him while looking for a place to pull off. This irregular driving continued for a while until we got to an intersection. He put on his blinker to turn but then suddenly pulled back in behind us. The warning signs continued to go off in my mind.

Shortly after the intersection, we drove on a road with mountains to the left and a steep drop-off of about 100 feet to the right. No room to navigate! Then he sped up, just missing the back of the bike, and passed around us on a curve, with little room to pass before any potential oncoming traffic. He passed and moved back into our lane, speeding up as he went around the corner and out of sight. There was finally some relief, but not for long.

As we approached the curve, I heard in my spirit, "Stop for the accident." *What!* I thought. Thoughts were rushing through my mind, and I wasn't sure what was going on!

As we came around the corner, I heard a loud crash and explosion and looked up to see the truck drive right into an asphalt machine with two large rollers, stationary along the left side of the road. The explosion only lasted a second without the truck catching fire. And two guys in motorcycles were headed toward us in our lane as they avoided a head-on collision with the truck. We all stopped in time to keep from colliding as panic raced across our faces.

We stopped and went to see the driver, who was not in good shape, barely alive with a twisted body. The engine was in the front seat passenger side, and everything in the back of the truck was thrown onto the mountainside. The driver must have hit the machine at 70 mph.

We were the first on the scene and called the highway patrol, who showed up a few minutes later. None of us could pull the guy out of the wreckage. We couldn't open any of the doors. The truck was a mess, and the driver was hardly breathing. Later, he died with paramedics on the scene.

One of the things I've learned in a time of need is to ask God two questions: "What is this about, and what do you want me to do?" It was appropriate for this situation. The answer was to share my faith with the other two men on bikes and standing behind me. I thought I heard God say, "It's too late for the guy in the car. Talk to the guys behind you!" I spoke with the two men and told them God had given them another day to live; they acknowledged the comment and said they hadn't been in church for a while. We talked a bit and then departed the scene after the trooper released us to go.

The next day we looked in the newspaper for any information that might lead to the trucker's erratic driving but could not get any resolution. The paper did record two deaths on that road. Someone else had died in another location.

"What was that about, Lord?" was my second question regarding the incident. I mulled it over for several days, and the answer I got was this: "The driver was trying to kill someone that day and ended up killing himself. It was not your day to die, and now you know the extent to which I go to protect you!"

The Lord is many things to us, but He surely is the great protector and will protect us from the enemy's schemes to kill, steal, and destroy until the day we go to be with Him. I find strength and comfort in this. It doesn't mean that we won't experience great conflict but having eyes to see and ears to hear matter.

OBSERVE WHO'S HURTING

People are never more ready to hear an encouraging word from God than when they are hurting. Usually, all we have to do is listen to their words to pick up on the possibility of anxiety or grief.

Whatever the case, when we anticipate God at work in the life of someone, all we have to do is show up, listen, and respond to the promptings from the Holy Spirit. This takes the pressure off of us and puts the burden on the One who is able to carry it. Powerful and effective ministry takes place in a natural flow of words, directed by God, specifically for someone else's needs.

My mother passed away several years ago from a stroke, and after her funeral, dad and I got into a conversation that led to a lot of negative, critical remarks from him. I knew he was hurting, so I listened and waited for a window to open to respond in love. His comments continued for a while, and then there was a pause. It was hard not to address his words, so I asked dad, "Can't you be less critical and more affirming of others?"

Out of his mouth popped, "I'd have to be born again to change."

I've come to realize there are moments in life when the supernatural presents to change a person. When dad said this, I responded enthusiastically with a big "YES!"

Immediately, he fired back, "No, not that Christian thing!"

Sadly, I let my dad intimidate me and got my eyes off of Heaven.

God presents Himself supernaturally in moments, and we need to be ready to respond and follow through. My dad had an opportunity that day to make a decision for Christ but passed it up in his anger. At his death in '21, I wasn't sure if he was a believer or not. Though he had gone to church his whole life, he did it out of respect for my mom, and I do not know if he had a relationship with Jesus. This incident with my dad made me determined to be more prepared for the next time God asked me to join His work and speak with more authority and power.

WALK THE TALK

Several years ago, the late and former owner of the Texas Rangers, Eddie Chills, said something very profound. He said, "It's not what people say that you listen to; you follow their actions. Their actions will tell you where their heart lay." Over the years, I have found this to be true.

My wife Janet came home from Bible Study Fellowship years ago with this statement, "Your walk talks, and your talk talks, but your walk talks louder than your talk talks." After my kids left the nest and got on their own, they told me that it wasn't what I said to them that was so influential, but what they saw me do that stuck with them. "Dad, it wasn't you preaching to us that made the difference; the way we saw you live was the difference." Availability and readiness to listen and see are two ways we can join God in His work.

PRAYER FOR OTHERS

Evangelist is one of the five-fold ministry gifts listed in scripture. Few of us have that "office of evangelist" calling, yet as believers, we are all called to share the Gospel and make disciples. When I was struggling over my role in this area of evangelizing, I was struck by a story shared with me by a woman in our office who was the widow of a former pastor. She communicated that she had been praying for a friend of her son, and she had made a journal entry about that prayer. Sometime after that entry in her journal and while the book was open, that boy walked by the book and noticed the writing. He was overwhelmed that she would think of him and pray for him.

Praying for others—even privately—can be evangelistic. Prayer is important and powerful and plays a role in evangelism. Prayer is just as important a part as the one standing up, making an altar call, or witnessing one on one. We can all participate in evangelism through this powerful means of ministry.

ENCOURAGEMENT

Encouragement can come in several ways. It can be a spoken word that breathes life into a person in the right moment, a hug, a smile, a message of support, or a Bible passage. It's not common to get these affirmations in this busy world. But when you need a word, and someone's there to give it, it matters!

I'm reminded of what Dick Howser said before my trade to Kansas City in January of '85. I was in Milwaukee with the Brewers at the time, and Howser said, "If we get Jim Sundberg, we will win the World Series." The Royals had a young pitching staff, and he believed if they got a veteran catcher to work with them, it would make the difference he was looking to attain. Dick must have been prophetic because, in October of '85, we were crowned World Champions. All year, those words stayed with me as we mounted several come-from-behind-positions to win the prize. There is nothing like words of encouragement. They refresh the spirit like water to a thirsty soul.

God speaks life into us as well! Four years ago, I was diagnosed with prostate cancer. Those initial words, "You have cancer," spoke volumes I didn't want to hear. Doctors cautioned me not to wait too long to take action. There were some aggressive cells. But more importantly, the words God spoke to me reversed all my concerns.

Moments before I entered the doctor's office to hear the news, I asked the Lord, "What is going on?"

In my spirit, God clearly spoke to me and said, "There's something there. but I got it!"

I had ten weeks of treatment in Loma Linda, California, and now four years later, there is no sign of cancer. Those words in my spirit held me throughout, even though I heard some discouraging words spoken by doctors. Through these past several years, I've been able to keep a positive attitude. One can bank on the words God speaks—they bring life!

I played for sixteen managers in sixteen MLB seasons and two of them twice. I had fourteen manager changes in sixteen years. Think about that! Only a few spoke words that made us want to play hard. When

I look back at my career, those who turned me loose and didn't micro-manage got the most out of me. Just a passing smile from the manager speaks loudly. Even a pat on the back went a long way.

We live in a world that often moves us toward thinking only of ourselves. It takes intentional compassion to think beyond ourselves to reach out and encourage others. And not just strangers we encounter; encouragement helps us build and strengthen important relationships.

———————— ● ● ● ————————

Offering timely encouragement sets up an element of trust and respect, and those lead to the opportunity to share Christ.

———————— ● ● ● ————————

After sharing my testimony for some forty-four years, I now see that offering encouragement is a tangible expression of my willingness to be available to God. People are encouraged when a Major League baseball player, who is supposed to have everything and need nothing, actually needs God like they do. They may not remember the details of my story, but they do remember that a baseball player loves the Lord and has a genuine pursuit of God.

There are many out there who need to see your love for the Lord demonstrated in your walk or through your words of encouragement. It is refreshing to love others through your kind words, and those kind words will make lasting impressions. It is good to minister through heartfelt words that reach down into their discouraged soul and lift them out to view the day from a higher plain. That higher plain will allow them to be more receptive to see the light of God that shines in your life.

UNRESOLVED CONFLICT/TIREDNESS

I cannot tell you how many times I have been thrown to and fro, back and forth in spiritual battles, because of unresolved conflict and, added on top, being tired at the end of the day. Sound familiar? I believe a lot of our difficulties can be avoided by anticipating when unresolved conflict and tiredness will cross paths. When they do, refuse to engage in a dialogue. That is a recipe for troubled waters.

There is a purpose to why God said in His Word, "Do not let the sun go down on your anger."[3] Unresolved conflict will often spin off as anger that will express its ugly head in a variety of ways. When we add unresolved issues to a difficult day at the office or the kids acting up for hours, it taps our reserve energies, which affects our state of readiness and our willingness to respond in the Spirit.

Just like you kick off your shoes at the end of a long day or when you are around the house relaxing, your "readiness" to witness or fight also has times to pause while you refresh and restore. No one sleeps with their boots on unless they are engaged in a fight. But being available to God, fully versed in the Gospel of Peace, your testimony at the forefront, and encouraging words flowing from your heart is part of your calling. It is a higher calling. Once we have these primary strategies of readiness mastered, we can take additional steps and go a little further in our understanding of readiness.

READINESS FOR SPIRITUAL WARFARE

ROOKIE

In sports, a rookie is a first-year player, untested and lacking experience at the higher levels of play. That doesn't mean that the rookie isn't capable of doing the job. In my first year in MLB, I roomed with another rookie, Mike Hargrove. As it turned out, we both competed against each other for Rookie of the Year, which Mike won. It was a head-to-head battle until the last month when the game load of 136 games got to me, and in September, my hitting diminished. We both held our own and contributed to a second-place finish for the Texas Rangers.

In the Christian setting, babies in Christ, new converts, or lukewarm people could fall into this "rookie" category—untested and lacking experience fighting the evil one. They might not even take spiritual warfare seriously, so they are vulnerable to the enemy's tactics. It may seem like every day is a battle to keep your head above water, never thinking twice about where the root of the adversity is coming from. Lack of readiness and little knowledge of the Word can put you at extreme risk of the hassles and fiery darts thrown your way. Not so with the seasoned believer who is in pursuit of spiritual maturity.

SEASONED

A veteran MLB catcher can sometimes go for 4 or 5 innings until he needs his protective gear. Sometimes he can go an entire game without taking a hit. Other times, a catcher can take a series of hits in a few innings that need ice applied to the area. Those hits get your attention, and you feel them for days. Some even need treatment to heal more quickly.

When I was in college, I had the opportunity to play games in the Yucatan Peninsula. I'll never forget the catcher on the other team only using a face mask, no chest protector, and no shin guards. The strange thing is that he caught the entire game without getting hit. Any hit to the body would have put him out of the game. Going without taking a hit is not likely in spiritual warfare. You have an enemy aiming for you. But take heart, Jesus won the battle, and so can you.

Seasoned soldiers are used to the weight of their gear. In time, armor becomes like a second skin. You are comfortable in it, and you might even forget you are wearing it. You may not really even notice minor blows from the enemy because your armor does its job so well. But now and again, a blow lands hard. This might be because the enemy aimed for an unprotected area, or it might be that the blow has such force behind it that it takes you unaware.

We don't notice a hit unless it hurts. At the moment of impact, we are alerted to an area of our life that is vulnerable to attack. Our first response should be, "What is this about, Lord?" and "What do you want me to do?" This posture makes an immediate, intimate connection to the One who knows all things and knows our pathway to diffuse the situation. Most attacks are just threats and small disturbances to steal our peace and joy. Major losses are different. And not every major loss is an attack of the enemy, but a major loss can weaken our faith and take much longer to recover. But when a blow hurts, shooting straight with the Father is our first place to go. Reaching out to others for support and prayer is next.[4] These actions bring healing and help us regain our freedom. Whatever the case, spiritual warfare needs our attention.

Let's now take some time to look at a state of alertness or readiness regarding spiritual warfare and connect it to some potential situations where it might occur. I will use myself to show you where you can anticipate spiritual attacks. For this exercise, I will use the same situations I shared in chapter two to show you the connection between hurtful experiences, their messages, and how the evil one might use them to affect your readiness to share the Gospel. This should help you make your own connections to determine what situations might allow a window of entry for the enemy.

FEAR OF FAILURE HINDERS WITNESSING

I cannot tell you how many times I did not share anything with a person for fear that I didn't know enough or that I would fail in some way to say the right words. This constant message in the back of my mind said,

"You don't know enough yet." The word "enough," which was associated with the experience as a ten-year-old, had crippling consequences on my life in many ways. One of those was that it affected my availability to be used by the Lord. Here is the sequence reworked for this section.

EXPERIENCE
10 years Old: 3 homeruns and 1 strikeout at a ballgame.

FALSE MESSAGE
*"You're not doing good **enough**."*

INITIAL INTERPRETATION
Failure.

SATAN'S FIERY DART
"You don't want to share with that person about God. You'll mess it up. You're not adequate for the task."

GOD'S PROTECTIVE SHIELD
"You don't have to be perfect. I'll give you the words. JUST SHOW UP—YOU CAN'T MESS UP!"

Another situation where a childhood incident colors the landscape of my life shows up to impact my relationship with my wife, Janet. Whenever she indicates to me in some way that I'm not doing something well enough. "Jim, all the weeds are not pulled," or "Jim, I told you to do a complete job of vacuuming the carpet; you missed some." If you direct these kinds of words to me at the end of a tiring day and I'm not alert, they can trigger a great lash back on my part that causes hurt. This kind of situation can also occur in other relationships wherever hard feelings go unresolved.

FEAR OF REJECTION HINDERS WITNESSING

Fear of rejection is another situation that restricts me from allowing God to use me to advance His Kingdom. Rejection is probably a bigger stronghold in my life than my fear of failure. Being a people pleaser, I want to be liked by everyone and the thought of someone rejecting me over my relationship with God was frightening. Let's look again at when I dropped the pass.

EXPERIENCE
Ninth Grade football game: dropped a pass.

FALSE MESSAGE
"I am accepted depending upon my performance."

INITIAL INTERPRETATION
Rejection.

SATAN'S FIERY DART
"You don't want to share with that person about God. They will reject you. You'll never see your friend again."

GOD'S PROTECTIVE SHIELD
*"They are not rejecting you. They are rejecting Me. I love you deeply. I will **never** reject you!"*

———— • • • ————

Rejection is God's redirection for you!

———— • • • ————

FEAR OF GOD'S WRATH HINDERS WITNESSING

I feared punishment from my father, and that fear led to an unhealthy fear of God. Recall the story where I shouted, "Sunny beach!" when I hit my thumb, and my dad punished me not for what I said but for what I was thinking when I said it. This incident resulted in a lifetime of performance-based attempts to earn approval and prevent disappointment or retribution.

EXPERIENCE
8 years old: Bicycle/Hurt Thumb/"Sunny Beach!"

FALSE MESSAGE
"There is something wrong with your behavior and how you think."

INITIAL INTERPRETATION
Blame

SATAN'S FIERY DART
"You don't want to share with that person about God. You will say the wrong thing and mess it up. God will not approve, and He will punish you."

GOD'S PROTECTIVE SHIELD
"There is no condemnation for those in Christ. I love you deeply, and I am proud of you! YOU ARE MY CHERISHED CHILD!"

I have come to realize that I cannot mess up a situation where God is drawing someone to Himself. I do not have the power to bring them to Christ; therefore, I do not have the power to push them away as long as I'm sensitive to Holy Spirit. If I say the wrong things, I will only give those looking for excuses the excuse they are looking for. If I say all the right things to a person, who is not seeking God or not yet ready to respond, they will find some other excuse to reject Christ. It is out of my control.

ENEMY'S TACTICS

DESTROY YOUR TESTIMONY

During the Persian Gulf War, I heard General Colin Powell talk about how to disrupt the enemy. He said, "In wartime, you bomb their bridges, take out their ability to communicate with each other, cut off their supply lines, isolate them from any of their resources, and then kill them." It doesn't get more direct.

In the spiritual realm, the campaigns against our testimony can have a similar flow where the evil one will try to cut us off from the support of others and isolate us until we make a mistake. Fortunately, it has been my observation that God's mercy, love, and grace often extended to us, seem to limit the damage, where our public credibility is allowed to show up for another day. I am grateful that I do not always experience the consequences to sin that I deserve.

However, there are less fortunate times when the enemy seems to have his way. There are times when people in all places of ministry have a major tumble. Where husband and wife, child and grandchild, presidents, cabinet officials, politicians, or the like, stumble to the dirt and get all bloodied. Behind this is a crafty adversary whose goal here is to strip believers of their credibility and discredit their testimony.

The enemy would like nothing better than to destroy your credibility to talk about God's faithfulness and goodness. He delights in the potential of a screw-up so severe that it not only dramatically affects the sinner but creates collateral damage, causing as much havoc as possible. This kind of compromise not only disrupts the present, but also puts the future in jeopardy as it tarnishes the integrity of the individual and their family. Even though God forgives the sinner, sin can have long-reaching consequences, affecting as many offsprings down the line as "to the third and fourth generations."[5] This is a high price to pay when a little restraint and discipline (and engaging God's power) could foil the attempt of the evil one.

The enemy would rather that we hang our head in shame in response to his harassment, distancing ourselves from God's forgiveness and love. That way, the evil one can isolate us even more and continue to apply his schemes to further us down the road of destruction. Once the enemy can isolate us, he can come in to do the real damage.

His damage is like that of a hurricane, which, after it has come through and done its thing, leaves destruction and devastation. The damage is widespread and takes a long time to clean up, but in most cases, the ravaged area is never the same again. This should stand as a warning to every saint in their short journey here on earth, not to be paranoid, but definitely to be on alert.

SUMMARY

READINESS TO JOIN GOD

We see God's power continuing to build in the life of a soldier for Christ as we lace up our Ready Shoes and move to pick up the Shield of Faith.

- **Belt of Truth**—the foundation of our relationship with Jesus that sets us up to pursue truth.

- **Breastplate of Righteousness**—applied truth about our identity and our position in Christ protects us from wounds and gives us safety to address past hurts and get set free from any strongholds.

- **Ready Shoes**—we are available to God, empowered and strengthened to testify to God's goodness, and we can stand fast in the Gospel of Peace with a solid footing.

God's truth (Belt of Truth) has connected us to an inner transformation by God's Word (Breastplate of Righteousness), which allows us greater freedom and power to testify and give glory to God (Ready Shoes—Feet Fitted with the Readiness of the Gospel of Peace). In the process, we arrive at benchmarks of faith and trust in Him (Shield of Faith).

As we track this progression in the armor, "Kingdom Building" has emerged as a central theme for applying the Shoes and Shield as both armor pieces reference a stance or posture of advancing God's Kingdom through testimony and acts of faith.

STEP UP TO THE PLATE

As you find a place to be alone and quiet for this exercise, listen to these two songs and let their words soak into your heart.

- "Heaven Come," Bethel Music by Jenn Johnson

- "Spirit Move," Lethal Music by Kalley Heiligenthal

1. Part of preparedness is being ready to speak—willing to share the Good News. **What is your testimony?** Take a moment to write down some part of your story that demonstrates God's love, mercy, and goodness in your life.

2. We learned that unresolved wounds or conflicts are entry points for the enemy that challenge your availability to be used by God. **What wounds or conflicts do you need to attend to?**

3. The enemy often confronts us with our credibility. Yet when we surrender our mistakes and character flaws to Jesus, these things no longer disqualify us. They become evidence of a living, loving, forgiving Father at work in our lives. **What part of your testimony is vulnerable to attack? Has this caused you to stop giving your testimony?**

4. Try this **Readiness Exercise**. Think through how a message from a previous hurtful circumstance might negatively affect your availability to join the Lord in His work. It is okay to use the same incidents you recorded in chapter two, or you might have different life events to process.

EXPERIENCE

FALSE MESSAGE

INITIAL INTERPRETATION

SATAN'S FIERY DART

GOD'S PROTECTIVE SHIELD

5. Try this **Relationship Exercise**. Think through how a message from a previous hurtful circumstance might negatively affect a close relationship in your life.

EXPERIENCE

FALSE MESSAGE

INITIAL INTERPRETATION

SATAN'S FIERY DART

GOD'S PROTECTIVE SHIELD

ENDNOTES

1. 1 Kings 19:11, NIV.
2. 1 Kings 19:11-12.
3. Ephesians 4:26.
4. Proverbs 27:17.
5. Deuteronomy 5:9, NIV.

Chapter Four
SHIELD OF FAITH

WHAT DOES THE SHIELD OF FAITH MEAN?
The Shield of Faith in place indicates that it is in God we trust.

WHY IS IT IMPORTANT?
Faith in God delivers hope to our hearts—it is His goodness, not our abilities, that shields and protects us from falling apart in difficult circumstances.

HOW DO I "PICK UP" THE SHIELD OF FAITH?
I say to God, "I believe; help me with my unbelief."

WHAT IS A TWO-WORD RESULT I CAN EXPECT FROM CARRYING THE SHIELD OF FAITH?
Unyielding Belief

WHAT ARE THE ENEMY'S TACTICS?
The enemy tries to create hopelessness in me. A hopeless heart cannot trust or believe in God's goodness and spirals into self-comfort, self-protection, and self-defense. This isolates me from my Father.

WHAT ROLE DOES CARRYING THE SHIELD OF FAITH PLAY IN SPIRITUAL MATURITY?

- *Faith pleases God.*

- *Hope is established in all other armor pieces.*

- *Unyielding belief—no matter the circumstances— creates the certainty of knowing.*

- *Faith destroys doubt and combats fear.*

- *We can lock shields with other believers for greater strength and strategy.*

- *Faith gives us ground to stand on and promises to hold onto so we can overcome hardship.*

SHIELD: GREAT CONFIDENCE

ACCOMPLISHED

My catcher's glove was my shield of faith. I could handle it as well as anyone with great confidence. Year in and year out, it was my steady defender. I won six consecutive gold gloves as the best catcher in the American League. Very seldom did a ball get past me. Currently, I'm third all-time in fielding percentage in MLB history, and only one error separates me from being the best. The only things that got past my glove were foul tips deflected by the hitter—until I started catching knuckleballer Charlie Hough.

You don't catch a knuckleball because of its unusual wobbling. A catcher wrestles it to the ground and waits for it to stop rolling, then throws it back to the pitcher. I even used a glove that was about 50% bigger for help. It's a nightmare to catch the knuckleball, and I had a few of them when I went to sleep. I never won another gold glove after catching Charlie Hough. Charlie said that I was pretty good at catching the dancing tumbler, but the balls getting past me increased to an abnormal amount for my liking. I started to have a crisis of belief where doubt and fear began to creep in. Soon I lost my confidence. I realized, however, that there was one person to trust in who would never fail. Life has situations where we move from unwavering faith to a faith crisis in a matter of moments.

IN GOD WE TRUST

OVERCOMING HARDSHIPS

When discussing the Breastplate of Righteousness, we looked at how childhood incidents color the landscape of our emotions. We can clearly observe how unresolved situations kick out distorted messages about ourselves and life. These messages target the heart of our emotions, especially before we knew Christ or as young believers were not able to identify and understand them. As we become spiritually mature, we learn to use our understanding of the Word and our relationship with the Lord to do something about those childhood hurts. When we address these issues, we can break free from whatever stronghold we are under.

As we move to pick up the Shield of Faith, we begin to respond to these occurrences as incidents that test our faith. These can range from losing a job to the death of a loved one to divorce from prolonged pain or illness to addressing our own mortality. These are life events that can have deep penetrating pain. They test the very fabric of our faith, but they can cause us to go deeper with an awesome and loving God. In these situations, God can bring a new revelation of Himself to us. Let me tell you a personal story.

In the early 80s, I was on the west coast preparing for a game against the Seattle Mariners when I received a call from my wife's obstetrician back home in Texas. "Jim, I'm sorry to have to tell you this, but Janet delivered a little girl this morning, and she didn't make it. I don't know what happened, but Janet is okay."

I got off the phone in a state of numbness with a flurry of thoughts running through my head, most of which started with the question, "Why?"

There are times when hardships occur where we get the opportunity to either run from God and hide or, in our grieving, embrace Him to find our way through it to deeper faith. Difficulty comes in many packages, but when we are willing to engage the Lord in our anguish and trust in Him, we will find the courage to go on.

After time has passed, we can usually look back on these events and see where God was faithful to us. When aligned with the promises in

His Word, these events can form a series of benchmarks that end up acting as pillars in our life. When new challenges come, we can reflect on these past situations for comfort. God's past faithfulness results in powerful experiences that help to sustain us through new challenges until the day we go to be with Him.

"I BELIEVE, HELP ME WITH MY UNBELIEF"

ENOUGH FAITH?

Faith is a constant thread of belief far more important than moods. Faith says stay the course long after a mood has passed. Faith is beyond feelings. It is based on a Greater Power outside ourselves. It is unyielding. Faith is the firm persuasion—"I know that I know" based on what God knows and who He is. Faith is not moved by changing circumstances because God is unchanging. Feelings come and go, but God is consistent, faithful, and removed from the see-saw of life happenings.

Faith stays the course long after a mood has passed

Sounds great, right? But how do we put on the Shield of Faith?

The Gospel of Mark gives us a clue. A boy was possessed by a spirit. Before Jesus heals him, the boy's father says, "I believe, help me with my unbelief."[1]

This is a terrific approach to putting on the Shield of Faith! This man's sincerity represents an unyielding pursuit to believe in God's ability, even when he was shaken. In essence, he says, "My faith is far from perfect. I may not have enough faith. If my faith is not enough, please help me have enough." Jesus was pleased with this response and healed the boy.

It is okay to say, "I believe in you, Lord. My pursuit to believe is unyielding, but I'm struggling a little with my faith; help me!" We all have a "faith crisis" now and again when we struggle to get our legs back under us while suffering as fear presses upon us.

FAITH CRISIS

I don't think anything causes a crisis of belief more than suffering—especially seasons of prolonged suffering. Prolonged suffering eats at the core of our belief in God's faithfulness.

I've dealt with depression at various stages in my life, and it's not any fun. I've often asked God to take it away and replace it with something physical, thinking that physical illness has got to be better than this mental anguish. Not great logic, but thinking logically doesn't come easy in the presence of illness. "Anything else but this, Lord," was my motto.

Early in my career, during an inactive offseason, I had to deal with a bout of depression. It was not until I read a book called *Adrenaline Addiction* that I understood what was going on with my body and mind. I would push myself so hard during the season due to fear of failure and trying to please others that I would deplete my system to the lowest level.

Because I would shut my body down by being inactive, depression would set in right after the season, even though rest was what I needed most. In reality, what the book said to do was phase my body down gradually with a little exercise instead of shutting it down cold turkey style. My body had become addicted to adrenaline, which I hit on every night in order to compete well and succeed. Shutting my system down by resting after the season sent it into withdrawal—just like from drug addiction.

Not only was I struggling physically with withdrawal, but add my unhealed childhood wounds to the mix, and I was a miserable person asking God why? Why did I have to go through such physical and emotional pain? Now that I'm on the other side of it, I've stopped asking why. God has been faithful and present the entire time—He never abandoned me.

As one who has suffered chronic depression, the best advice I can offer if you struggle with this is to be careful about putting so much emphasis on your feelings. Yes, emotions need to be addressed but not consume you. It's hard to do, though. I am not making light of how heavy they are and how hard it is to shift your gaze. Know that the depression will pass, and take heart if you're struggling.

Depression is a signal of something not working. There was a physical cause and an emotional element in my case. Through counseling, the work of the Holy Spirit to teach me about a loving Heavenly Father, and the proper use of medication, I have been able to endure the episodes until they passed.

You are not alone if you're struggling with a faith crisis. It happens more often than you might expect. God is faithful and promises never to abandon us. Any crisis of belief generally has a good dose of fear coming from different directions and messaging.

FAITH DESTROYS FEAR

The Kansas City Royals were the first team in MLB history to come back from a three to one deficit in games played post-season and managed this feat in both the playoffs against Toronto and in the World Series against the Cardinals. I survived the fear of losing by counterbalancing it with an attitude that there are worse things that can occur than losing. Faith continues tomorrow because it's bigger than fear.

Trailing three games to one, the atmosphere in the locker room prior to Game Five of the World Series was palpable—focused. I didn't see fear in the eyes of my teammates, only the quiet confidence of taking one game at a time with a relentless focus on winning Game Five.

Danny Jackson was superb that night, defeating the Cardinals in St. Louis to send it home for Game Six. Danny had a lot of guts—there was no fear in that kid—and he put the St. Louis club on its heels with the victory.

Franklin D. Roosevelt once said, "The only thing to fear is fear itself." Fear can be paralyzing, but that night, there was only the hope of another tomorrow with a win today. Fear is like a monster; if you give it an inch, it can inflate into full-blown panic. There was no panic that night in the locker room before the game.

The Kansas City Royals of '85 took that fifth game victory home, and in front of an enthusiastic crowd, we went on to win Games Six and Seven for the title. Fear of losing was laid to the side because, as professional athletes, we knew the dangers of such a negative influence.

In a recent Bible study, I came across this paragraph that works well for many situations:

> *How do we fight this inflated monster? We face it down with truth. If there's a big threat hanging over our head, take a good hard look at it. Ask yourself, what is the worst that could happen? What adjustments would I need to make if it did happen? and Could I live with those adjustments? Play the whole scenario out in detail in your mind. By exposing the inflated fear to actual reality, you'll discover that even the worst possibility is far less damaging than the fear of that possibility. As a result, the fear begins to shrink to a manageable size. It begins to lose its icy grip over your heart and turns into something that you can handle.*

The enemy of this world loves to use fear to paralyze people. He knows that God's protection is a powerful tool against this fear. Once you realize that going to Jesus is a safe place, you can handle whatever hardships come your way. Even the worst scenarios have a way of working themselves out. The Royals knew we could lose because our opponent was good, but we managed to become World Champions through the deficit. We knew that choosing the right perspective allowed the best of our abilities to flourish.

No matter your situation—work, home, and everyday stresses—choosing faith over fear matters.

FEAR IS NOT YOUR MASTER

My baseball career challenged me to confront my fears. I'm glad there were no other options other than to tackle the fears. One of my worst was the fear of flying—it gave me gut-wrenching, white-knuckle trauma. I had to conquer it or quit baseball. The stakes were too high to quit. I knew there was no reason to be afraid, but I was. That's how fear works. But there have been numerous others I've had to breakthrough in order to survive and live with a greater sense of freedom. Fear is not your master unless you agree to become its slave. We must move forward in the face of fear and not run from it. The goal of never being afraid is unrealistic. It's not the absence of fear but moving forward with the presence of fear is how you conquer it.

It takes courage to move in the face of paralyzing fear. There is freedom on the other side for those who navigate these waters. In the Bible, there are 365 "fear not" scriptures signifying a warning. Fear is a major emotion the enemy can use to stop someone in the tracks. I don't believe there is any other emotion mentioned more than fear. Fear stands in opposition to faith and makes you feel hopeless. Faith delivers hope.

FAITH DELIVERS HOPE

GOING DEEPER

Let's look at how the Shield of Faith and the Breastplate of Righteousness can be viewed as pieces of armor that support each other—protecting the heart and delivering hope. They work together to thwart the strongest attempts of the evil one to bring a Christian down.

We have talked about the messages that come from unreconciled childhood events that can follow us into adulthood and cause great insecurity. We are now getting into situations that can cause tremendous grief as adults. You can see how overwhelming events can be when you mix your unreconciled past with a new traumatic event.

I want to look at some situations where the enemy waits in hiding to utilize his tricks, even though he may or may not be directly involved in causing them. I will take ideal situations from the enemy's viewpoint and run them through the window of the Shield of Faith and the Breastplate of Righteousness with the diagram that follows.

When the enemy uses failure, rejection, blame, and shame, he tests our understanding of our position in Christ. We answer these with the Breastplate of Righteousness. When the enemy uses loss—financial failure, lost romance, illness (loss of health), job loss, divorce, death, etc., he is testing the depth of our trust in God. We combat this with the Shield of Faith.

I believe that the fiery darts hitting the Shield of Faith are easier to handle when our foundational position in Christ (Breastplate of Righteousness) is understood and in place.

Whenever there is an attack by the enemy, we are invited to go deeper into our relationship with the Lord. It's encouraging to know that God is in control when our faith is being tested and that God can use evil to draw us closer to Him. This brings us to that most precious word called hope.

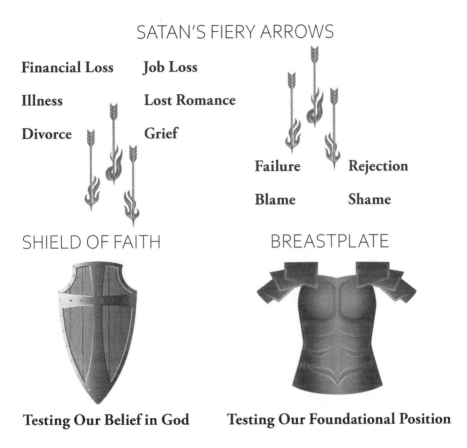

SATAN'S FIERY ARROWS

Financial Loss   **Job Loss**

Illness   **Lost Romance**

Divorce   **Grief**

Failure   **Rejection**

Blame   **Shame**

SHIELD OF FAITH

Testing Our Belief in God

BREASTPLATE

Testing Our Foundational Position

EMOTIONS

Hope

UNYIELDING BELIEF

MAKE MY STAND

When you look at the words "unyielding belief" side-by-side, perseverance pops up. You are said to be unyielding when your heels are dug in and you are not going anywhere. "Here I am, and here I'll stay! There isn't anything you can do to uproot me from this place! My feelings may not match up at the time, but they will catch up! If you come to get me, you better be prepared to take no prisoners." You will find this attitude in a person who is unyielding.

I remember driving along the Mississippi River in Illinois after one of the worst floods. Later, I was watching television, and the interviewer asked a man, "Why was it that he would go back to the same area and rebuild his home again?"

The man responded, "This is where I'm from; this is what I know. There is no other place to go."

This man's clear resolve illustrates an unyielding belief in Christ.

When things get messy, we are confronted with two options. We can take flight and run from our problems, become angry and withdrawn from God and others, or confront them and allow God to do a work of craftsmanship in our character. In his book, *The Silence of Adam*, Dr. Larry Crabb says:

> *No man can escape the sphere of mystery. If he lives in relationship and has any desire at all for the relationship to work, he will face unsolvable confusion. If a man is to be fully a man, he must learn what it means to move in darkness. And that will require*

him to admit "I don't know what to do" with a despair so real that no recipe will help.

Recipes are useful in a well-lighted kitchen. Recipe theology, that collection of practical biblical principles that tell us what to do in every situation, treats confusion as something to be solved rather than entered. It reduces the mysteries of life to things we can manage.

Recipe theologians tell us how to make life work by simplifying things and relieving confusion. Transcendent theologians know there is a darkness of confusion that can only be entered by knowing Christ, by abiding in Him, by trusting Him to supply supernatural power to hover over whatever darkness we face, and then by moving into that darkness with words that bring life.

All of us have seen the well-meaning Christian with their collage of pat answers in their attempt to bring relief to a hurting friend or relative. I could also be accused of administering this same type of support at one time. The older I've gotten and the more experiences I have had, though, brings me to this same place on the road as Larry Crabb. At times, there are no easy answers to life's journey. We may have to enter incredible darkness with unyielding belief if we are to be resurrected in the newness of life.

Sometimes it is as if God has become silent, waiting for our confusion to become so intense that we will know without any doubt that it is He who is bringing us out of our darkness and back to life. In this darkness, we have no other option but to draw nearer to God, to rely on His supernatural power to sustain us in the darkness, and then revive us in His timing. Engaging the Lord in these times develops an unyielding belief in God's ability to provide during our darkest hours.

BUILDING AN UNWAVERING LINE OF DEFENSE

CERTAINTY OF KNOWING

During my ninth year in the majors, I had the privilege of catching Charlie Hough—remember, he was that knuckleball pitcher. I was known for my outstanding defensive ability. Whatever I did with my glove or arm was very effective. I learned to develop great confidence in my throwing and the use of my glove. To a catcher, catching was second nature, like brushing your teeth at night before bedtime. But you didn't catch Charlie! To be his receiver was the worst experience I had in the majors because it stripped me of what I could do best, what I had gained enormous confidence in my ability to accomplish.

That life experience made me realize that some circumstances and situations are out of our control and call upon us to recognize a power bigger than ourselves, where our confidence is shattered. These circumstances signal us to look to build an unwavering line of defense, a certainty of knowing. This starts with our relationship with Jesus (Belt of Truth) and the truth of His Word (Sword of the Spirit). We take those elements into our vulnerable places (Breastplate) and begin to find a sense of freedom. We develop relationships with people we can be authentic and honest with, which aids in our healing process.[2]

BETTER TOGETHER: LOCKING SHIELDS

In an early scene of the movie *Gladiator*, well-trained soldiers are advancing together side-by-side against an untrained barbaric enemy. What caught my attention was how impenetrable the Roman guard was to the fiery arrows of the adversary. Whenever the enemy shot their arrows into the air against the elite guard, the good guys would drop down in unison, lifting their shields to protect themselves from head to toe, from front row to back row. This illustration gives us several points to demonstrate what we have at our disposal to build an unwavering line of defense to fight spiritual warfare.

In the movie, you could observe the well-trained Roman soldiers purposely collapsing together, all in formation, covering their bodies from top to bottom with their shields to block enemy arrows. When I see this, I'm reminded of the importance that loved ones and friends play in times of crisis.

• • •

The enemy would like nothing better than to isolate you from any source of support and then stoke the fires of loneliness and despair.

• • •

It took me a long time to let down my pride and open up about painful emotions. For years I stayed in emotional isolation and seclusion from others. God's Word is very clear when it comes to effective prayer—where two or more are gathered, so shall I be there.[3] This one took me a long time to use!

One of the biggest breakthroughs I experienced came when I started to lock shields (engage) with other believers. John Weber was the first close male friend I ever had, which wasn't until the late 70s. John was on staff with Athletes in Action and was in charge of the chapel and Bible study programs for the Texas Rangers and the Dallas Cowboys. God began to open me up emotionally in a safe and loving environment through this man.

Others would come into my life over the next several years, and in 1984, I put together a life Board of Directors. These eight people would later have a significant impact by praying for me during the World Series the following year. There were some incredible God moments in that series for me, only because of that step of faith by having them pray. God seems to supernaturally work in greater ways when groups of His children lock their Shields of Faith together for one another. When the most difficult situations occur, you do not want to enter them in isolation without this locking of shields. What a terrific way to experience the Lord and His unwavering line of defense!

CAIRNS—LANDMARKS TO RECALL GOD'S FAITHFULNESS

CONFIDENCE IN DIRECTION

We go to Colorado several times a year to visit and stay with my wife's sister in Winter Park. Many of those trips were spent hiking numerous trails, and there are markers to guide travelers from one major point to another. These tall guideposts are not needed so much in the summer but are helpful in the hard winter when the snow is high. These cairns, as they are called, give direction in the midst of what could be terrible conditions to a weary traveler. Cairns serve as markers providing confidence to the traveler on what direction or pathway to go. They keep the person on track to get to their destination.

Confidence in something or someone is usually based on trust stemming from a satisfying or favorable experience. A good track record creates an assurance of something good to come.

In the spiritual realm, faith markers are moments where God has shown His faithfulness. We can always use those experiences to remind us of His trustworthiness during another battle. Previous God moments keep us hopeful and encouraged that we will come through our next challenge.[4]

A relationship with Christ creates an expectation of something good yet to come, even when something bad has happened. God is the only One who has the credibility to be trusted and faithful. When we have had a series of experiences with God that has proven His faithfulness, they build our confidence in God that can be used to get us from one adverse condition and back on the right trail.

The Old Testament is interspersed with stories of God's faithfulness to Israel. When we read His Word, we come to realize, as believers, that we can draw on the same promises and expectations of God's deliverance as did the Jewish nation of old. When we begin to record our own experiences of God's provision to us, they serve as powerful spiritual markers similar to those recorded in the Bible.

I have created ten such markers in my life, but I will share three with you. I will offer a short synopsis of each event and then ways in which God showed His faithfulness that continues to be real even today.

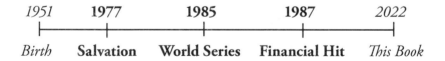

1951	**1977**	**1985**	**1987**	*2022*
Birth	**Salvation**	**World Series**	**Financial Hit**	*This Book*

MARKER #1—SALVATION

I shared before how I grew up in church but without meaning. As an adult, nothing satisfied my soul, and there was a deep void not filled even by the successes, luxuries, and limelight of my MLB career.

I was somewhat frustrated by parts of my performance. I won the first of my Gold Gloves for outstanding defensive ability, but still, my hitting left much to be desired. In 1977, I was on the verge of losing my job as new manager Billy Hunter took over.

Out of my professional frustration and the continuing ache from the major void in my life, I was open to looking back at my church roots to see if I had missed something. Through the help of a relief pitcher on my team, I realized that I was missing out on a personal relationship with Christ. I had known religion, but I did not know about a personal and intimate relationship with God.

In June of 1977, the Lord moved to bring me into His Kingdom in my hotel room in Toronto, Canada. After a game, I came to know Christ as Lord and Savior when I got on my knees to receive Him into my life. Things changed forever!

How God Displayed His Faithfulness

1. **God wanted To win my heart.** God has continually won my depraved heart over and over again as He reminds me of what He has done. He showed me that in a relationship with Him, I had supernatural ability to reach my fullest potential in my career.

   After becoming a Christian, my game excelled. Over the next five years, I performed at the highest levels. God met me at the place of my greatest need to get my attention and win my heart. He has never stopped!

2. **I met the Holy Spirit.** This is the most precious gift of all, and the Spirit worked to guide, correct, direct, comfort, encourage, and love me. He sealed me for eternity, and nothing can take that away.

MARKER #2—WORLD SERIES CHAMPIONSHIP

I always wanted to play in and win a World Series. This happened in 1985— after much blood, sweat, and tears. Before that amazing day, I first learned what it was like to be out of favor with the team. In 1983 my Texas Rangers manager made it so difficult that I was dying to leave after the season. I didn't think I ever wanted to play baseball again. If I hadn't had three more years left on a lucrative contract and a family relying on me to provide for them, I might have quit. It was that bad!

By the start of the following year, I was playing for the Milwaukee Brewers, and by the middle of the year, I was a member of the 1984 A.L. All-Star Team and fully recovered emotionally. I regained my confidence and desire to play out my contract and maybe even further. I eventually played for the Kansas City Royals, and my childhood dream came true—World Series Champion!

How God Displayed His Faithfulness

1. **All things work together for good.** When I was going through the ordeal during my last two years in Texas, I often asked the Lord, "Why?" After being traded to Milwaukee, I had a great year and then found management wanting to trade me. Again, "God, why?" By the time I got to the end of the 1985 season, I sang praises to the Lord and no longer asked my question.

    I realize now that God wanted something better for me than I could see or imagine at the time. At one point in Texas, my roots were so embedded that it took a succession of two new managers, two new general managers, some influential teammates with ownership, and two years of fighting off gossip, to root me out of Texas. God used them for the greater good in my life. It took THREE YEARS for me to see it!

The Lord developed my character to trust and rely on Him—more deeply winning my heart and showing me that a relationship with Him had the potential to make all things work together for my good.

2. **Discipline is God's place.** During that last year in Texas, I publicly remained silent about how I felt regarding my treatment and the manager. Oh, I told Janet and the Lord about my distaste for his public ridicules, and I complained in private areas. People would say, "Why don't you stick up for yourself and let him have it in the papers?" But I kept silent.

   I read the scripture saying, "Revenge is mine, says the Lord."[5] I knew God would go before me and be my banner; I didn't need to lash back. I trusted He would set the record straight for me, restore my credibility and respect, and set me high upon a rock. I could trust that He would fight my battles.

   After having the All-Star year in Milwaukee and after the Rangers had a chance to see their replacement for me, they were ready to get me back. God had restored my credibility. The Rangers took so much flack from fans for trading me that after the 1984 season, ownership met privately with me to try and talk me into coming back to Texas. After numerous meetings, I rejected the kind gesture and moved on to Kansas City.

   When it came down to it, the manager who made so much trouble for me really had no control in my life. He was only a vessel God used in my journey at a time to demonstrate His faithfulness to me.

MARKER #3—FINANCIAL HIT

Traumatic events rock the soul. You can get so discouraged that words cannot communicate your grief. Janet and I lost a baby, and we've each now lost both of our parents. In 1987, I had a financial hit that penetrated my soul in ways never before touched because we had the possibility of losing everything we had labored for in baseball.

I met a man who gained my confidence over two years. On the heels of winning the World Championship, while acting as my agent, investor, and friend, this man came off the elevator in the stadium and had me sign some papers. We later followed that up with a few more documents in a formal setting. Just like that, I was in a real estate project in Austin, Texas. Yeah, you savvy Texas real estate people of the 80s know what's coming!

I knew it was a real estate project, and I was told that my liability would be around $300,000. I could accept that level of responsibility. I didn't know that my investor, agent, friend, seminary graduate, first in his finance and business class, the one I trusted, didn't tell me that my exposure was in excess of $2 million! I didn't know that the real estate market was getting soft and that he was using this project to bail out another one. It would be six months before I heard anything, and that was via the grapevine. Within two years, I lost $1 Million.

I played the last few years of my career with that impending financial crisis over my head and the possibility of leaving baseball after many years with nothing. I fought depression, anxiety, and panic attacks. The betrayal of the deep personal violation from a very close friend was intense. I asked the Lord, "Why in the world did you put me with this guy?" and "For what purpose is this, Lord?" I had planned to save everything and use it in ministry without having difficulty raising funds like I had seen friends do. I was devastated.

How God Displayed His Faithfulness

1. **The Lord is the one true source to trust.** I remember telling this agent friend, "I trust you so much I don't know what I'd do if something bad happened." I learned the hard way that there was only one person that I could trust with my heart, and that was Christ.

   In the process, I realized a valuable principle that gives me freedom today. Man is sinful, and when backed into a corner, he will protect himself and those close to him. I no longer put unrealistic expectations on others, and I have been able to extend grace never present before.

   The Shield of Faith has blocked the enemy's fiery darts many times. "The Lord is the stronghold of my life—of whom shall I be afraid?"[6] When the rubber hits the road, only God is worthy of my full devotion and trust.

2. **God keeps my ego in check.** Before signing the papers to be involved in the project, I sat in my accountant's office discussing the possible consequences if things went bad. I actually said, "I can handle a $300,000 loss; in fact, I could take a $1 million hit!"

   Well, if you have been following closely, you realize why I have never forgotten that statement. That is exactly, almost to the penny, the losses I incurred. Besides the emotional trauma, Janet's loss of confidence in my ability to provide is still occasionally used today by the enemy to cause discord between us.

   When my ego rises, the Holy Spirit quickly reminds me of that incident long ago. I am grateful to have a companion living within me to guide me when my flesh wells up with pride.

3. **Mistakes allow us to grow.** Before the early '80s, I usually wanted someone else to take care of me. I didn't want to make any major decisions nor put forth much effort on anything outside of being in uniform. Most players do not even want to talk about the end of their careers. Most believe that if they make enough money, they will be okay. Out of fear, I moved forward with the Austin project, and I delegated the responsibility of decision-making to this agent, investor, and friend.

I learned that no one looks after you better than you! Yes, God causes things to work together for good, and He does look out for our well-being. But He expects us to listen to Him. He gave us free will to pursue things of our choosing.

No one looks after you better than you!

This experience taught me to pursue only those things that I know and can perform. If the Lord hasn't gifted me to do it and I'm unwilling to put the energy into it myself, I do not participate. This attitude led me into a successful business experience that has taught me so much and now paves the way for my next phase in business.

The essence of responsibility is doing well with what God has gifted you to do, listening to Him, waiting on Him (sometimes withholding your impulses), and trusting Him to provide (faith).

4. **The Lord restores.** It is so exciting when one has come full circle to see the blessings of Christ. Hardship is difficult to endure, but for those who keep their eyes looking up and endure, much will come forth to praise God for His goodness.

This Austin project involved a group of all Christians, some twenty-five people. When it started to go bad, everybody bailed—some left town, others responsible went into hiding; some hid behind attorneys and left the responsibility to work through the problem with me. I was the least knowledgeable person in the group about the project, but as it turned out, I had the most exposure with the most money for the bank to go after, and after it, they did!

At one point, it looked as if I would be responsible for the whole $3.5 Million project, and that would have bankrupted us. As my attorneys got involved, they advised me that the liability would be much less than originally thought but would be very costly. In trying to be responsible and handle it in a Christian way, I hired a good Dallas law firm that determined my real exposure. I paid the money and responded with integrity by not chasing my Christian partners in court, nor the bank who did some squirrelly manipulating of documents, and so I moved on.

One of the neatest outcomes of this mess was God's continual faithfulness to me. I believe God honored me by the way I took responsibility, and He replenished the entire amount and more. He did it through a good tax refund and a two-year extension on my playing career.

The Lord is an awesome God who wants our heart, in its present condition, to mold in His ever-loving hands. I would not be the person I am today without having experienced the above situations and more. I believe that because of these experiences, I am a more rounded person. I have learned to trust Him more deeply, had my heart softened toward Him and others in the process, learned to be more responsible in my life with what He has given me, and I have a genuine desire to know and pursue Him.

God's eternal life, love, forgiveness, and grace are all free to us. The peace that comes from a deep trust in God is earned through the knocks of life while in a relationship with Him. I wouldn't take back those incidents and what they taught me for anything.

ENEMY'S TACTIC

CREATE HOPELESSNESS

One of the most troubling realizations I made during one of the darkest periods of my life is that a Christian can be in an emotionally worse situation during conflict than a non-believer. Yes, you heard me correctly; now, let me explain.

When I was a non-believer and found myself in a really bad situation, there was always the thought in the back of my mind, "If I turned to God with this, He could probably make it better, but I won't play that card right now."

During the Austin real estate ordeal, I got so depressed—anxiety and panic attacks set in—that for the first time, I really understood hopelessness.

I was a Christian, praying for God's deliverance amid the worst emotional state I had ever been in, but God did not appear to respond. This anguish lasted so long that I just wanted to go to be with the Lord and avoid the conflict. Death sounded like a good way out.

I could not think clearly anymore. I felt like even God couldn't help me. I kept saying to myself, " "I'm a Christian, and God is working in my life. Only He can do the impossible. It might take some time, but He is capable of making this work for my good."

Christians are not immune to desperation. If we are not fully equipped in God's Armor, we are susceptible to the enemy's tactics. I have known

a few Christian men who took their own lives, and I know what it is like to be on that edge of hopelessness.

The enemy attacked me with a series of lies, and through those, he worked under stealth, gradually moving me deeper into a rut. God was also working in my life by using this period to re-shape my thinking and heart. He used my situation to reach me in a way that I began to pursue Him, desiring to be a man after His own heart. God does not cause evil, but He can use evil and the evil one to shape us into His image. God is in control of everything.

I eventually responded to the Lord's direction and found my way out of the muck. In the process, though, I gained a deeper understanding of what Christ's death and the resurrection were all about.

The advantage for the believer is that when they have come through their trauma, they can access the power of the resurrection when confronting the enemy. These people make good friends to know when fighting spiritual warfare. They have seen the enemy face to face and survived it to join God as a true warrior in Christ. I am forever thankful to know Christ in this way.

Yes, the enemy has God's permission to have access to His children. The Book of Job tells us this, as does Jesus when He says to Peter, "Simon, Simon, Satan has asked to sift you as wheat."[7] The enemy will use whatever we give him to try and disrupt our faith in God. He will try to entertain us with doubt and fear in the hopes that it can lead us to anxiety. Once anxiety sets in, depression and panic have a chance to take root. If depression and anxiety find their way with us, hopelessness can set in. If hopelessness sets in, we will find ourselves in real trouble.

We need to prevent this sequence of hopelessness by picking up the Shield of Faith. When doubt and fear are introduced, before Satan has the opportunity to set up a stronghold, we arm ourselves with the Shield of Faith to block his fiery arrows. Even if the enemy gets through, God is capable of bringing us through our darkest moments.

SUMMARY

HOPE IS PRESENT IN ALL ARMOR PIECES

Hope should be a constant theme for the Christian. It is like the polish on your armor. Your faith creates the hope to walk through life as a conqueror. *Webster's 1828 Dictionary* defines hope as "a desire of some good, accompanied with at least a slight expectation of obtaining it, or a belief that it is obtainable."

Webster continues, "Hope differs from wish and desire in this, that it implies some expectation of obtaining the good desired, or the possibility of possessing it. Hope, therefore, always gives pleasure or joy; whereas wish and desire may produce or be accompanied with pain and anxiety." Wow—what a great word picture of hope!

Webster was also onto something from a spiritual standpoint when he further defined hope as **"confidence in a future event; the highest degree of well-founded expectation of good; as a hope founded on God's gracious promises!"**

Okay, let's review:

- Putting on the **Ready Shoes** communicates that an internal transformation has taken place in our life as a believer. This peace readies us to join God in His work—spreading the Gospel. We are **always armed.**

- As we pick up the **Shield of Faith**, we hold onto our trust in God, His goodness, and His providence to work all things— even difficult and traumatic ones—for our good. He uses these situations to deepen our faith. We have an **unyielding belief.**

- With our Ready Shoes and Shield of Faith working together, we advance the Kingdom of God **around us** and **within us** through deeper faith.

- **Hope** is the constant thread linking all armor pieces together.

- When you truly connect the significance of these two armor pieces and apply them, you are willing and desiring to **submit to God** by pursuing the road to Christ-likeness.

The Helmet of Salvation is the next piece of armor we will study and examine how our thought processes affect the road toward sanctification.

STEP UP TO THE PLATE

As you find a place to be alone and quiet for this exercise, listen to these two songs and let their words soak into your heart.

- *No Longer Slaves*, Bethel Music by Jonathan Helser, Joel Case, and Brian Johnson

- *Hope's Anthem*, Bethel Music by William Matthews and Christa Black Gifford

In the exercise following, you can record your top three experiences that are your own faith markers. I encourage you not to stop at three but continue this exercise in a journal. Rehearsing these milestones of God's faithfulness is one way to pick up the Shield of Faith.

EXPERIENCE	DATE

HOW DID GOD DISPLAY HIS FAITHFULNESS?

EXPERIENCE	DATE

HOW DID GOD DISPLAY HIS FAITHFULNESS?

EXPERIENCE	DATE

HOW DID GOD DISPLAY HIS FAITHFULNESS?

ENDNOTES

1　Mark 9:24.
2　James 5:16.
3　Matthew 18:20.
4　Romans 8:28.
5　Romans 12:19.
6　Psalm 27:1, NIV.
7　Luke 22:31, NIV.

Seasoned Warrior

HELMET OF SALVATION

SWORD OF THE SPIRIT

A s we become seasoned warriors, much of our spiritual battles will transition from direct attacks of the enemy into a mental exercise of discipline and strategy. By now you have recognized that an intimate relationship with God is the single most important factor that keeps you on course. The journey has been tough, but as a believer, you surrender your will to God and trust Him for the best plan. Because you understand Christ's love and acceptance, you develop the desire to bring every thought and situation to God. Consider the WWJD movement from the 1990s, where we started asking, "What Would Jesus Do?" in a situation. We can approach our thoughts with the question, "Is this thought pleasing to God?"

Putting on the Helmet of Salvation and wielding the Sword of the Spirit involves patience. You must pursue Christ and then wait to receive a word from Him. That word might be a verse or passage of scripture that the Spirit quickens to your mind where you will find peace, comfort, or a promise to stand on to counter the attacks of the adversary. Whatever the need, when you wear the full Armor of God, you are a special forces agent—disciplined, committed, and knowing the Word of God and how to use it effectively.

Chapter 5
HELMET OF SALVATION

WHAT DOES THE HELMET OF SALVATION MEAN?

Wearing the Helmet of Salvation indicates you have engaged in the battle to have a mind like Christ.

WHY IS IT IMPORTANT?

Our mind is where we exercise free will. Our life is the sum of our choices, and great choices require that we renew our minds with the washing of the water of the Word and make decisions fully aware of the sacrifice Christ made for our salvation.

HOW DO I "PUT ON" THE HELMET OF SALVATION?

I put on the Helmet of Salvation when I manage my thoughts and choose to do what Jesus would do (WWJD).

WHAT IS A TWO-WORD RESULT I CAN EXPECT FROM WEARING THE HELMET OF SALVATION?

Love Rules

WHAT ARE THE ENEMY'S TACTICS?

The enemy comes to steal, kill, and destroy our destiny. One of his main weapons is deception—he tempted Eve with knowledge—the arena of the mind and making choices. His chief ploy is to compromise our thought life.

WHAT ROLE DOES WEARING THE HELMET OF SALVATION PLAY IN SPIRITUAL MATURITY?

- *We gain a disciplined mind—able to take thoughts captive and meditate on Him.*

- *We have the mind of Christ; therefore, make better choices.*

- *We understand we are on the road to sanctification—it is a process.*

- *As we submit to God, the devil flees from us.*

- *We walk in grace, aware and on guard against the enemy's tactics to deceive.*

HELMET: RIGHT CHOICES

DOWN, NOT OUT

Around 1980, I was hit in the head hard enough to earn a three-day hospital stay. The blow knocked me out for a few seconds before I gained consciousness. If the same thing had happened to a Roman soldier, it would have meant death. A soldier knocked out would be run through with a sword. Thankfully, I was more fortunate. I couldn't move or even think, rendered helpless as I lay on the ground. If the mind is incapable of working, nothing else can. Without a helmet, I could have received worse wounds or even have been killed. Instead, I received a small concussion and was back in action a few days later.

Once I regained my wits, I could answer the trainer's questions so we could make the right choices about what to do next. The mind is where we exercise our will. It is our command central, where we make decisions—good or bad. So, what can cause a person to make decisions contrary to their base nature? What causes us to follow something or submit our will to someone else? Unless love and trust are involved, submission is hard.

BUY-IN: A CASE FOR LOVE AND TRUST

SUBMISSION

Submission is not easy to discuss because it's counter to our nature, which wants to do whatever we want to do, whenever we want to do it.

We have seen that wounds can cause us not to trust. Wounds will keep us from trusting until they have been healed and reconciled by Jesus. I believe the armor pieces have a progression to them, an order for how we put them on. By the time you successfully navigate to this point in understanding and applying the armor, you love and trust in the only One who can deliver. Then submitting to Him and making good decisions become second nature.

My experiences have led me to believe that given the right circumstances, no human heart is completely safe with another human— even those we love and trust. It's possible for me to hurt my wife, and my wife is capable of hurting me, and the same goes for other relationships. No human is capable of holding a heart as well as God or of loving the way He loves. God is Love, and He is trustworthy.

We must choose to submit as an act of our will. If we choose this regularly, we develop a discipline toward submission. This discipline can lead us to make the right choices and responses in following a wonderful God. One way to develop submission is to keep the phrase, "What Would Jesus Do?" (WWJD) close at hand.

The seasoned Christian mindset is willing to submit to the authority of Christ. This means you have come to believe God's love has no bounds. You have to buy in to the truth that He is faithful and trustworthy. This does not come without a battle!

LOVE RULES

One of the most powerful words in the world, if not the most powerful word, is love. "Love makes the world go round," as they say. Even those who do not believe in God agree that "All we need to do is love one another" as the cure to the world's problems. Love is powerful, and you will find it hard to locate anyone who thinks differently.

For the Christian, love should become the motivator for everything we do; not guilt, not fear of rejection or failure, but our love for Christ. He first loved us. From that love, we develop our love for Him and a trust that makes us willing to submit to Him.

Behind religious activity comes the need to perform. It says, "Since I do not have an intimate relationship with God and do not know how He will receive me, I must fall back on what I know and what the world tells me—I must perform to be accepted." Under this scenario, the Christian walk becomes a bunch of do's and don'ts that you can check off. Your performance gauges your level of spirituality. The very thing we try to overcome with this strategy is the very thing we end up failing to do— prove that we are right with God.

In an intimate relationship with God, we come to understand His Word and receive it at face value. We are fully persuaded that Christ's death on the cross was enough to pay for man's separation from God. We know that those who receive Christ as Lord and Savior are loved, totally pleasing, fully accepted, and complete in Christ. We need nothing else to be righteous before God. When our understanding of God's deep love for us is made complete in our heart, we become overwhelmed with the Lord's goodness. We desire a life of integrity (as salvation plays itself out), submitting to the Lord's leading. At this point, the love of God rules in our heart.

SEASONED WARRIOR

BATTLE FOR A DISCIPLINED MIND

Discipline is not the most popular word because it implies great effort and a personal battle of the will. There is nothing lazy about discipline. It encourages us to withhold something for later, while our desire for immediate gratification or advantage often wins out. When we give in to these desires and abandon the disciplines we have put in place, we break the commitment we made to ourselves and sometimes to others.

We must have a realistic goal in mind. Something we can see that our exercise of discipline will get us there. The motivation to be disciplined comes from the belief that doing this difficult thing right now will result in a future reward. My ability to maintain discipline sets the table for that great reward. The required discipline must be realistic enough to always keep the future reward in sight. Once the possibility of receiving that reward is reduced, we begin to lose motivation. Once motivation is lost, the likelihood of receiving that reward is diminished.

It's easy to look at a military uniform and see the discipline and commitment of a soldier. The same was true in Roman times. The uniform of a Roman soldier communicated many things suggesting discipline of purpose, sacrifice, and service. Here are a few examples of what a military uniform communicates:

- Name
- Rank
- Branch of Service
- Campaigns Served
- Years of Service (in some cases)
- Operation Specialty
- Awards/Medals Won
- Recognition
- Schools Accomplished
- Tenure (or Volume of Experience)
- Combat vs. Non-Combat

In other words, a veteran soldier is a model of a disciplined mind. The decorations on a military uniform show rank. For the Christian, one way of thinking of this is by the stripes that have been healed—our testimony, the sacrifice we have made for the Kingdom of God, and what is written about us in the Lamb's Book of Life. None of which come easy except to the degree a mind is yielded to Christ.

Some time ago, I was on my way to the office and running a little late. You know, I got caught in some traffic and was running behind to get to work and start the day. I was making a right-hand turn but had to yield to the left for oncoming traffic. There is always this little Indy driver inside me that says, "You can beat them if you step on it!" The yield sign means that I am supposed to slow down, pause for oncoming traffic if necessary, and wait until the appropriate time to continue. The battle of the mind on the road to Christ-likeness is much like this traffic incident.

I have found the struggle in my relationship with God similar to what happens at this type of intersection. Part of me doesn't want to slow down, be quiet, and wait for the Lord. That rebellious side would much rather try to get in front of God's timing, not yield to Him, and risk being in dangerous territory without the Lord at my side.

The road to becoming more like Christ requires the discipline to pause and listen to God, yield yourself to His will and timing, and realize that His direction is the best way to live. This yielding of our will to God's will brings us down this glorious road toward a disciplined mind.

ROAD TO SANCTIFICATION

When we receive Christ, we receive salvation. The transaction is instant. We once were lost, but now we're found. Sanctification is the process of how we "live out our salvation." The day we are saved by God's free gift is just the starting point of our relationship with Christ. Once saved, we start down this road with Christ (to live out our salvation). To be sanctified requires submission to God, a continuous surrender of our will for His. That lifestyle of surrender is possible only when our love for Him exceeds our love of self.

The road to sanctification and a baseball player's career have many things in common. There is a starting point (salvation) when the player begins to play baseball at a young age (infant stage). A lot of passion and discipline goes into becoming more skilled (mature). Years are spent fine-tuning the mind and body while keeping an eye on the goal, a longing to become MLB players (Christ-like). Along the way, there are many successes and celebrations, setbacks and failures, and seasons of difficulty where slumps are longer than desired (hardships). Other times see periods of great success (favor and blessings), periods of adjustments required to further the career (journey), and consistency of play for the veteran (seasoned warrior).

Induction into the Hall of Fame for the believer happens when we finish our race here on Earth and join Jesus for eternity. As long as we breathe, our journey stretches before us—there is no destination, only stops along the way and the joy of traveling. A disciplined mind leads the way.

When a hitter steps up to the plate, it becomes a battle of the mind to stay focused on the task of having a good plate appearance. There are obviously physical elements in play with your swing, but much of the battle to thwart outside distractions and internal negative messages happens in the mind. Yogi Berra, known for his colorful quotes, once said, "Baseball is 90 percent mental. The other half is physical." Hitting is a mental battle to stay in the sweet spot to get a hit. An All-Star hitter fails seven out of ten times. In Christianity, when we fail to hit the mark, grace abounds.

— • • • —

It is a relief to know when we fail, God's grace allows us to get up, dust off our clothes, and keep swinging.

GRACE ABOUNDS

We can't wear out grace—it abounds! That's not to say we should take advantage of grace. Grace isn't a magic button to push to keep us from accepting responsibility. A seasoned believer doesn't desire to take advantage of grace or cheapen it in any way. Believers understand the price Jesus paid for us to have that grace, so we move to honor God in all we do. Then when we fail, we accept the grace given. I don't buy into the church's fast food definition of grace as simply "unmerited favor!" This definition doesn't work in John 1:14 when it says that "Jesus ... was full of grace." How could Jesus be full of unmerited favor? So, this definition doesn't come close to explaining its meaning.

Years ago, I heard a better explanation that said **grace is God's empowering presence in a person's life to be and to do.** This definition opens it up for the fullness of grace's meaning:

- God working through us to love others,
- to forgive others while receiving mercy and forgiveness ourselves,
- to step into everything God is and present that to others,
- to be empowered in ministry,
- to stand as a son or daughter of the King of Kings,
- to be favored and blessed,
- to be worthy of the calling,
- to be everything God intended,
- to be and do as God commands, and if not, then to be covered by the blood.

Grace is everything God is and wants to be and do for us ... and more than we can imagine.

THE MIND OF CHRIST

INTENTIONAL PURSUIT

How can anyone grasp the mind of Christ? How can we truly know what Jesus thinks? The only way to begin to know the mind of Christ is to know the Word of God and intentionally move toward Him. In the next chapter, we will get more into the Word of God (Sword of the Spirit).

The Bible teaches that the longer we are Christians, the more our love for Christ grows, and with that deeper love comes our consistent submission. The world we live in—this period of eternity— is difficult. Evil is on the rise; sin and fear are prominent. But now, just as throughout history, the indwelling Holy Spirit does battle against our inner rebellious flesh nature and our tricky adversary.

I liken the Helmet of Salvation to the catcher's mask and helmet for a baseball player. In the same way, they serve as protective gear like the Roman soldier's helmet. In my career, baseballs from the bat of a hitter deflected and hit my mask hard enough to interrupt my ability to think. Looking back on those experiences, I realized that I could not mentally process anything or enter into decision-making in that dazed state of mind.

The Helmet of Salvation is about the battle of the mind and the will of a believer. By protecting your mind with God's Word and submitting to God, you will have a life of abundance, even while experiencing hardship. The essence of life and its successes are based on our responses to God's invitations. An empowered godly life ultimately comes down to intentionally desiring the mind of Christ. We have to give everything in this lifestyle.

OUR LIFE IS THE SUM OF OUR CHOICES

RIGHT CHOICES/BAD CHOICES

As I shared earlier, in the early days of my walk with the Lord, Janet and I were at a professional athlete's conference at the Campus Crusade headquarters. A story was shared about a staff member who had an affair with a close associate and how it devastated the family and disappointed many people around them. How could that possibly happen to a person in leadership who has a relationship with Christ? It was unsettling to my soul.

At that conference, an explanation was given that made sense, and I have never forgotten it. "Temptation is like getting into a canoe upstream where the waters are quiet and easy to navigate. You don't know that there might be trouble right around the bend. But the thrill of the ride gradually pulls you downstream until you realize you're in trouble, and either you can't row to the shore to get out, or maybe you don't want to get out anymore."

It gradually became clear to me how much we live in a fallen world and the reality of an extremely crafty adversary. It is not difficult to get yourself into trouble. The landscape is cluttered with people, in and out of the ministry, who have put their reputation, family, and future in deep waters because of an irresponsible act of selfishness. Usually, behind this act is a period of being out of fellowship with the Lord and His Word and isolating from others. That sets the stage for vulnerability. With a little forethought and the discipline to keep yourself out of harm's way, you can respond in a way that honors Christ.

The seasoned warrior is sensitive to these potentially troubled waters and remains disciplined to row to the shores to get out of this dangerous river of compromise. Meditating on God's Word is an important discipline. One goal to keep in mind is to hear the words, "You were good and faithful. A job well done—enter into My presence!"[1] A desire to be better develops at the core of a seasoned believer to honor God in all He does. This drives us to be diligent in applying the Helmet of Salvation and constantly renewing our mind.

RIGHT CHOICES

We must choose to follow Christ. Will we follow Christ or our flesh? Will we discipline our minds and take those thoughts against God's knowledge captive to obey Christ? Will we recognize the source of our thoughts and be able to discern what is from the Holy Spirit and what has demonic influence? If we realize demonic influence in our thinking, we must allow the Holy Spirit to counter those thoughts with truth and God's Word.

If we do not choose to follow Christ on the front end of a compromising thought, we open ourselves up for a gradual ride down that river of compromise. The further down the road we get, the more difficult it becomes to get free of those thought patterns. Unchecked thought patterns eventually turn into actions, and actions turn into destructive behavior that, in turn, leaves a trail of pain and confusion.

BETTER MATTERS

Life is hard, sometimes rough, with obstacles to overcome. It's good to have good people around you to make you a better person and challenge you to make good choices. Iron does sharpen iron! My wife Janet motivates me to be better because that's who she is. She has always had higher standards. She raised three kids with high standards—not including yours truly as the fourth kid! My amazing wife sharpens me! She is a gift from above.

It's important to be around people who are better because they make you want to be better. I ended up with the opportunity and pleasure of catching eight Hall of Fame pitchers. They each made me better!

Ferguson Jenkins and Greg Maddox had the best control. Both may very well go down in history as the best control artists of all time. Catching them elevated my game behind the plate. Game calling (making choices) becomes simple when you work with guys who hit their spots.

If you needed to win a game, Fergie wanted the ball. On the last day of the 1974 season, Jim Bibby was supposed to start but got sick and had to sit out. Some thought since his record was 19-19, he didn't want to take the chance of losing 20 games. So, after three days of rest, Fergie took the mound and won his 25th game of the year.

Maddux couldn't throw a ball straight; everything moved to the right part of the plate with the precision of a brain surgeon. He once analyzed his game, saying, "The ball came out of my hand wrong five times." He could recall each moment the ball wasn't just right in his hand.

Nolan Ryan had the best fastball, curveball combination, and he was a tough pitcher. He and Burt Blyleven were one and two with a great breaking pitch. Nolan had seven no-hitters, but more impressive was his 42, two-hitters or less. Everyone knew that if he was getting his curveball over the plate for strikes, you were in trouble. In my collection of baseballs, I have his 5010th strike-out ball in my office. The significance of that ball is that my number was ten, so he gave it to me—a testimony to his character. I also had the privilege of working with him in the front office for six years while winning the AL championship in 2010 and 2011—the best years the Rangers have had.

Gaylord Perry was the toughest competitor. He would wrestle his grandmother to the ground to win a game. And he did throw the spitter. Kept K-Y Jelly on his neck. After a pitch, he would load up by swiping

169

his neck with his fingers on his follow-through. He never admitted to me that he threw the spitter, but my glove communicated something different.

Don Sutton was also a great pitcher. He knew himself better than anyone. Don knew when he didn't have any more to give and wasn't shy to tell the manager. Some criticized him for taking himself out of some games, but I never held that against him. A manager never really had to decide to pull him from a game. He made the choice. Don knew when it was time and let the manager know it. I respected Don for that example. He taught me a lot of things about responsibility.

Rollie Fingers and Lee Smith were great closers; very consistent day in and day out. They were one-inning guys who could close the door on any team. Rollie was rough around the edges; he could be a jerk but was a great competitor. Lee Smith would sleep in the clubhouse for five innings, then slowly make his way to the bullpen in about the 8th inning. It might have taken him 10 minutes to walk from dugout to bullpen in Chicago that was no farther than 50 yards; that's how slow he walked.

Jamie Moyer is the lone guy not yet in the Hall of Fame, but he has a chance. He was the off-speed master at locating the ball—spotting his mediocre fastball wherever he wanted, backing it up with sinker and change-up. He had an okay curveball which he used as his third or fourth pitch. I loved catching him because you had to use strategy with him, mixing pitches and keeping hitters off-balance. I used my experiences from all the other pitchers and helped teach him how to pitch. He thanks me every time I see him.

Just like my relationship with better ballplayers did, my relationship with Jesus makes me want to be better, too, and the Holy Spirit guides me in the direction of what Jesus would do.

THOUGHT MANAGEMENT

WHAT WOULD JESUS DO?

In today's business culture, we have many terms that communicate the importance of management—personal management, time management, total quality management, fitness management, etc. The one area of management we do not give much time to is thought management.

We have all seen the bracelets worn by people sporting WWJD (What Would Jesus Do) on them. When they first came out, I was just beginning to apply this piece of armor and was blown away when I saw those bracelets being worn by so many. I have come to recognize this simple phrase as the best way to "put on" or "apply" the Helmet of Salvation.

The Helmet of Salvation is our connector to God throughout the day when we do not have time to drop on our knees in prayer. It becomes a way to access the Lord in quietness through our thoughts. We can utilize this in the course of a conversation with a friend, during a drive in the car, in a meeting or conference room, by quietly asking the Lord, "What would you do in this situation? What wisdom can You give me? How could I glorify You? What could I say that would give this saint encouragement?" When I first began to approach the Lord quietly in my thoughts, I had a really neat discovery of how it works.

REACT OR RESPOND?

Several years ago, I was in an accountability group with two other men. The three of us had casually been talking, and then the conversation shifted to some heavy stuff where one of the men confessed something he was still engaged in. The more I listened, the more I began to wrestle with disgust internally. Then it struck me that this might be a good time to exercise the idea of what the Helmet of Salvation suggests we do in situations like this. It actually becomes another form of prayer that is extremely powerful. It does not take the place of our quiet-time prayer with the Lord, for all prayer should evolve from that time.

As I was listening, I chose not to react but to respond by talking to the Lord through my thoughts, by first confessing to the Lord that I did not have it within myself to help this person without His intervention in my emotions. I felt like reacting by punching him, but that was not the Lord's style. I confessed my inadequacy in having words to express to my friend that would make my friend listen to and respond appropriately. While the third friend talked with him, I remained quiet, bringing my thoughts before the Lord in private. It was actually amazing that I went as long as I did without saying anything, but engaging the Lord allowed me the power to do so.

> *I chose not to react but to respond by talking to the Lord through my thoughts*

About five minutes went by as I continued to connect with the Lord while listening to my two friends, wondering if I would end up saying anything. Regardless of my emotions with the desire to wrestle my friend to the ground, I desired to be able to receive from the Lord and do what He wanted me to do, and in His timing. A few more minutes went by, and suddenly, there was a lull in the dialogue. As quickly as the pause in the conversation came, so did the words out of my mouth, and they were not of me. I mean, it was one of the most amazing moments of conversation that I have ever had—and to top it off, he listened.

RESPONDING

Submit ⟶ Resist ⟶ Wait ⟶ God's Response

The above process is one of the most effective tools we have at our disposal to do ministry, enhance job effectiveness, improve relationships, and fight spiritual warfare. When we are willing to submit our thoughts to the Lord, no matter how bad we may think those thoughts might be, God can do amazing things through that person for everybody's good. Managing our thoughts is a discipline. By asking Jesus, "What would you do in this situation?" we can live an effective life that allows us a better chance to make the right choices at the right time for ourselves and for the Kingdom of God.

RIVER OF COMPROMISE

SLOW FADE

I talked about how our thought processes can move us gradually down the river of compromise if we do not cut off dishonoring thoughts and allow them to gain momentum. It's a slow fade! Recall that I shared about someone in ministry who became entangled in a sexual relationship with an employee who devastated his family and ministry. I want to discuss how a person in such a leadership position can get caught up in a web of deceit that leads to destruction.

I will use the diagram that follows to give you checkpoints to help you recognize where the critical crossroads exist. There is no magic in these descriptions. They are here as one method to help you better navigate those bends in the river. At the end of the chapter, you will have the opportunity to look at an issue that is difficult for you and map out a strategy to avoid the river of compromise and its slow fade.

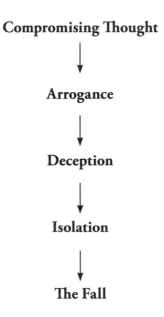

Compromising Thought

↓

Arrogance

↓

Deception

↓

Isolation

↓

The Fall

COMPROMISING THOUGHT

Everyone has fallen short of the glory of God. There is no one who hasn't had a compromising thought run through their mind. The Bible lists a whole bunch of sinful behaviors—lying, sexual immorality, cheating, stealing, killing, dishonest gain, and so on—that first take root in the mind and, once manifested there, move to an outward action. Since sexual immorality is a leading cause for people to stumble, for this exercise, let's look at how this path might look. Although men and women arrive differently at this place of vulnerability, they both still arrive with similar thoughts due to a worsening relationship with their spouse.

STAGE 1: INITIAL THOUGHT

"That person is really attractive. It would be fun to talk to them and get to know them."

This thought is not sin. It is impossible to go through life without seeing others we think are attractive. However, if the casual glace goes beyond just noticing that someone is attractive, resulting in an action toward them, then the thought has taken root, and compromise has begun.

Arrogance

The pull of temptation's current begins as the person starts to make their way down the river. At this point, it is a stream and not yet the rapid waters of a raging river. The stream could also be looked at as the river of sin. Because of our sin nature, we find ourselves in the river relying on the hope that God's redeeming power will rescue us every day. It is easy to navigate upstream where the waters are calm, and the scenery is beautiful and peaceful. It's hard to imagine that there might be trouble around the bend.

STAGE 2: ARROGANCE

"This is really fun to play these visual and verbal romantic games. I know it's wrong, but I still have time to get out before it's too late."

There are many little games of words that two people attracted to each other can play. It is almost like fishing, in that one person throws a topwater lure out there to see how the other will respond. Something like, "I've decided to leave my spouse," or "My spouse ignores me," or "They treat me so badly." This can be used to see how the other person reacts—if they'll take the bait and respond with affirmation or sympathy. If so, then both have accelerated the depth and speed of the water down the river.

Deception

At this point in the river, it is becoming harder to take to the shore where relief (our relationship with God, His Word, and friends who hold us accountable) might be found. The thrill of the ride (romantic jostling) is exhilarating. Because of the speed of the water (progression of the emotional attachment), it gets harder to manage the boat (desire). This is very close to the point of no return.

STAGE 3: DECEPTION

"This feels too good to be wrong. I can't believe that a loving God would want me to hold back on something that seems so right for us."

Feelings are important to understand and recognize for our emotional well-being. But feelings do not take precedence over what the Word of God says about our relationship with others while married. Adultery is wrong regardless of what we think our feelings are saying about right and wrong. Feelings can be very misleading and cause us to be deceived by the evil one. This kind of deception can move us down the river of compromise through this slow fade, where we run from conviction into the comfort of isolation.

Isolation (Shame)

When Adam and Eve sinned in the garden, one of the first things they did was to go and hide. They tried to isolate themselves and run from God because of their shame. At this point, the need to hide meant that they knew they had done wrong, and they were moving into darkness with their guilt. Their sin now had tremendous power over them.

Now back to our example. Once deceived into believing their actions are justified, we see the relationship take them into another phase toward destruction. The couple begins to meet privately. Sneaking around is a dead giveaway that they know they are wrong, so they meet secretly and hide the shame. They are now running from the reality of the devastation that is just around the corner.

STAGE 4: ISOLATION (SHAME)

"I'd better be careful that no one finds out about this. If we can keep this a secret for a while, we'll figure things out."

There is nothing worse for keeping a person in bondage and living a life with no power to overcome adversity than to keep something a secret! I have heard horrible stories where family members are told that if something got outside the family, then daddy would lose his job, or his position in the church or community would be hindered. Their kids eventually grow up with a chance to be a basket case, dealing with the incongruency and hypocrisy, continuously struggling with life. Defeat seems to be their constant companion.

The Fall

Once they begin meeting in secret, physical intimacy is the next step. Their minds justify behavior they know is wrong because it meets a need or serves to punish a spouse perceived as lacking. The more they justify their actions, the harder they work to keep things secret, and the more deeply rooted they become in their sin. They have basically given up their family for the thrills of certain desires that will fade as quickly as the relationship. Destruction of relationship, emotional pain, and the loss of God's blessing awaits their every move from this point forward.

STAGE 5: THE FALL

"I really do not care anymore."

The Word of God says that He is faithful and will not let you be tempted beyond what you can bear but will also provide a way out.[2] As we apply this verse to the river of compromise, we see a person gradually move down the calm waters of a stream where an early exit is the easiest place to leave. But they don't take the prodding of the Spirit and continue to move downstream where the current is briskly moving. The Lord continues to prod them, showing them the danger of their behavior and offering a way to escape, but they choose to remain in the river, heading for turbulent waters without listening. Now it is difficult to get out, and most likely, there is no desire to leave. So they get carried away in the current, head over the falls to the destruction of their family, the dismay of their friends, the possibility of job difficulties, and the loss of integrity.

The way to stop this gradual decline to ruin is to know where you are in the river and take action while still in the calm waters upstream. Confess your need for the Lord and ask for His forgiveness. Expose temptation to the light of others' ears. Once exposed, it generally loses its power. Our love for God motivates us to confess our faults and pray for healing. When we desire His Lordship, we can say, "Create in me a clean heart, O God, and renew a steadfast spirit within me."[3] Love for the Lord should rule in the life of a believer.

ENEMY'S TACTIC

MOVE US TO COMPROMISE OUR THOUGHT LIFE

Back in the early 90s, I struggled with depression. My internal systems were worn out, and I was tired of them running at a high pitch of performance. I had gotten to this point gradually across time, where I had bought into some of the deceitful lies of the enemy centered around the need to be liked, to receive approval, and the fear of failure, all associated with perfectionism.

It was as if God allowed me to continue down this road as an approval addict in a performance trap until I arrived at that point where I finally got it. Only God knows where that point exists for each of us, and the journey is painful—especially if you hit rock bottom.

***

Most of us do not join God in the reshaping of false messages into healthy ones unless and until we experience pain.

***

The enemy knows our weak points, so it only makes sense that we become familiar with them also. If you have been caught in a performance trap, one of the enemy's strategies might be to get you to think you are not saved or loved by God. Salvation is a free gift and cannot be earned on good behavior. But a person in performance mode takes a while before they really connect with the fact that their performance has nothing to do with their salvation. Some patterns of thought are so deeply embedded that it takes a total collision with that misguided thought pattern before it is purged from the believer and a new thought pattern is born.

God cannot cause evil because it is not in His character to do so, but He can use the evil attempts of the enemy as well as any circumstance we find ourselves in to bring about a healthy shape to our thinking. God is always with us, and He uses even the work of the enemy to touch areas where we are vulnerable. Through this process of being hassled, God invites us to join Him in reshaping new and better messages that reform our thinking into the image of Christ.

I believe that once a person has received Christ, they cannot be indwelled by a demonic spirit like a non-believer can. I have always been taught that the Holy Spirit and a demonic presence cannot dwell together in the same body; that the temple of the Holy Spirit cannot share the same space as the evil one or his comrades. Others believe that this is possible for the Christian who has strayed far away from their relationship with God. Continually living in sin allows the enemy more and more territory in their life until it opens this door. There is very little comfort for the believer in the thought that an evil spirit can indwell them and scripture teaches differently. If it were possible, it should then stand as a warning to believers who consistently live in sin. For the purpose of this text, I want to address the first one.

If it is true that evil spirits cannot indwell a believer, then the influence of demonic activity must come from outside the person. First, the flesh is capable of wrongdoing on its own. The flesh does not need much encouragement to indulge itself in sin. In Romans, Paul talks about the sin nature and the battle he had with his flesh. The flesh is like a young child, who naturally, on his own, does not pursue responsibility and is easily influenced by anything that comes along. Like a child, the flesh needs to be trained into obedience, or as Paul says, "But [like a boxer] I strictly discipline my body and make it my slave, so that, after I have preached [the Gospel] to others, I myself will not somehow be disqualified [as unfit for service]."[4] So from this point of view, we can assume that our sin nature (flesh) can easily be influenced by outside sources, whether it is delivered through another person or directly from an evil influence.

SUMMARY

BRIDGING SUBMISSION WITH THE WORD OF GOD

The Word of God is our ready defense against every lie of the enemy. It is a pure source for encouragement, instruction, wisdom, and counsel. The Helmet of Salvation protects our thought life—the place where we exercise our free will to choose or reject God. Our thoughts become our actions, so shielding and protecting our mind from the world, the flesh, and the devil is critical to our Christian walk.

You may have heard the statement, "The Word works for those who work the Word." Submission to the Lord—and to His Word—is a choice. We submit as children with a free will, born out of our love for God and trust in His goodness.

As we transition from the Helmet of Salvation to the Sword of the Spirit, let's take a moment to review the order we put on God's armor by summarizing each with a two-word description.

BELT OF TRUTH—**SET FREE**

BREASTPLATE OF RIGHTEOUSNESS—**HEART RESCUE**

READY SHOES—**OUR TESTIMONY**

SHIELD OF FAITH—**UNYIELDING BELIEF**

HELMET OF SALVATION—**CHOOSING RIGHT**

If you have armed yourself with all these armor pieces, you are not a passive Christian. It is not an easy journey to get to this point of discipline and submission. Much territory has been covered. You are becoming a seasoned warrior, and though the price is high, the reward is great.

The Helmet of Salvation and the Sword of the Spirit are best used for seasoned soldiers in Christ. Seasoned soldiers know how to fight the good fight against the forces of darkness and their flesh nature. In this process of advancing through the armor, hands-on training has been invaluable.

In the next chapter, we'll explore the Sword of the Spirit and get you ready for the front lines. Now more than ever, you will see how valuable it is to apply the Word of God to live a victorious life in Christ.

STEP UP TO THE PLATE

As you find a place to be alone and quiet for this exercise, listen to these two songs and let their words soak into your heart.

- *What if I Gave Everything?* Casting Crowns by Bernie Herms, Mark Hall, and Matthew West

- *I Surrender (Remix)* by Hillsong Young & Free

Following is a series of questions you can ask yourself to determine if you are in the river of compromise and, if so, at what stage. Know that rescue is just one prayer away.

STAGE 1: RECOGNIZE A COMPROMISING THOUGHT
UPSTREAM/CALM WATERS/EVERYONE HAS BEEN HERE

1. Has there been a thought continually on my mind?

2. Is that thought associated with a potential sinful act?

3. Am I attracted to the possibility of its fulfillment?

STAGE 2: ARROGANCE
SCENERY IS BEAUTIFUL/WATERS ARE BRISK/INVITING

1. Is there a desire to play around the edges
    by taking this thought into action?

2. Do you find yourself believing you are in control and
    have the power to get out when you think you need to?

3. Do you find yourself saying, "I am in control; a
    major incident could never happen to me"?

STAGE 3: DECEPTION
THE THRILL IS GREAT/THE RIVER IS FAST/EXCITING

1. Are feelings becoming the guiding light
    for your actions vs. God's Word?

2. Do you speak to yourself saying things like, "This
    feels too right to be wrong," or "A loving God will
    be gracious to me!" and justifying your behavior?

3. Is your fellowship with the Lord broken off?

STAGE 4: ISOLATION
CANOE OUT OF CONTROL/THE RAPIDS/IN OVER YOUR HEAD

1. Do you find yourself moving into
    secrecy with your actions?

2. Are you concerned that someone will find
    out about what you are doing?

3. Do you make up excuses to cover your tracks?

STAGE 5: THE FALL
HEADED ACROSS THE WATERFALL/BIG DROP/DEVASTATING

1. Has sin manifested itself on a regular basis?

2. Do you find yourself not caring for what was, at one time, a very important value?

3. Do you wonder about your salvation?

ENDNOTES

1. Matthew 25:21.
2. 1 Corinthians 10:13.
3. Psalm 51:1.
4. 1 Corinthians 9:27.

Chapter 6
SWORD OF THE SPIRIT

WHAT DOES THE SWORD OF THE SPIRIT MEAN?
Wielding the Sword of the Spirit allows us to deploy a strategic strike against the enemy with God's Word.

WHY IS IT IMPORTANT?
More than just knowing the Word of God, using the Sword of the Spirit is the active engagement of a believer with the Word. It indicates we have a deeper understanding and helps us gain an advantage over the schemes of the evil one.

HOW DO I WIELD THE SWORD OF THE SPIRIT?
I wield the Sword of the Spirit when I target specific verses to specific needs. I come into agreement with the principles and promises of God found in His Word.

WHAT TWO-WORD RESULT CAN I EXPECT FROM USING THE SWORD OF THE SPIRIT?
Our Edge

WHAT ARE THE ENEMY'S TACTICS?
The enemy is a liar. Sometimes his lies are outright and obvious. Sometimes he puts a more subtle spin on truth, knowing that even a little deception gives him a foothold in our life.

WHAT ROLE DOES WIELDING THE SWORD OF THE SPIRIT PLAY IN SPIRITUAL MATURITY?

- *The Sword is not just a protective, defensive weapon. Using the Sword allows us to be proactive and go on the offense as well. We can take territory!*

- *It allows us to apply a specific verse to a specific need.*

- *We can personalize how we interact with the Word, utilizing our unique learning style.*

- *Like soldiers running drills, we must practice using the Sword of the Spirit regularly to remain sharp, ready for battle, and fit for service.*

- *It is like curating a "personal playlist" of the truth of the Word.*

SWORD: STRATEGIC STRIKE WITH GOD'S WORD

SPECIFIC VERSES TO SPECIFIC NEEDS

In your mind's eye, picture a Major League Baseball player and his bat. Now, apply this imagery to a seasoned believer and the Word of God. Both have an adversary who is trying to conquer them by using some sort of strategy. The baseball player and the believer both need to become skilled at using their "weapon" to counter the opponent's work and strategically strike at the appropriate time. We do this by applying a specific verse from God's Word to a specific need to counter the enemy.

A player can order his bats to a customized length and weight, designed just for him. He can even prescribe the type of treatment given to the outside of the bat. In other words, the bat is made especially for the individual so he can use it most effectively. The same is true for the Bible; it is designed and written by God for our effective use.

From the time a baseball player leaves the dugout and approaches the batter's box in preparation to hit, he is beginning to formulate a strategy against the pitcher based on knowledge of his opponent correlating with an assessment of his own skill. The hitter must also be aware of past situations in which the opponent exposed a weakness and be watchful for any opportunity to capitalize on flaws the pitcher may exhibit. This attack and counter-attack posturing go on throughout a player's entire career. The ones who learn to focus on the reality of the game-day situations and can make the appropriate adjustments have the best chance of success.

In the early part of my career, before becoming a Christian, I remember carrying my Bible with me on road trips as a good luck charm. I seemed to draw some comfort by having it in my suitcase, but I never opened it up. After becoming a believer, I gradually started reading it regularly, but it wasn't until about three years into my relationship with Christ that I really began to study and make application. The Sword of the Spirit is the Word of God; however, I believe that the implication of this piece of armor is deeper. The Word was intended not to be just looked at but to be known well enough to be applied in the life of a child of God.

The Word of God and the Holy Spirit have a similar relationship as a computer's hard drive with its stored memory. While the computer's shell represents a person's body, the hard drive and its memory represent the Holy Spirit. Once a believer, the Holy Spirit has the capacity to store memory (God's Word). In this illustration, you can easily see the importance of studying the Word of God to apply it. Like a computer accessing its hard drive, the Holy Spirit accesses what the believer has stored from their study. This is not to say the Holy Spirit is limited to what we know and understand, but He has greater interaction with us when we know how to listen, and there is a greater capacity with those who read and know the Word.

OFFENSIVE / DEFENSIVE

Most people realize that the Word of God and a baseball player's bat are offensive weapons. The player uses his bat to crash against a ball when the pitcher has delivered a mistake. Likewise, a believer takes action against the adversary when the enemy delivers a fiery arrow (thought, message, or action) by using God's Word to counter. Both the Sword of the Spirit and the bat can become defensive weapons.

Wade Boggs was one of the best hitters of all time in Major League Baseball and a Hall of Famer. I would readily tell my pitchers that I knew how to get two strikes on him. "Just throw your first two fastballs on the outside part of the plate," I would tell them, "and you'll have two strikes." Wade would not swing at the first two pitches if they were on the outside corner. The problem, though, was that he was the best two-strike hitter in the 80s and 90s.

He was the best because he could wait until the last moment and "fight off" difficult pitches (deflect the ball into foul territory) until the pitcher made a mistake, and then he would rifle the ball somewhere for a hit. Wade could wear down a pitcher until he made the error and then make him pay for it. This "fighting-off" of a pitch is known as defensive posturing, which normally occurs until the hitter gets back to an offensive position (the count even or in his favor) to attack the ball (Satan's darts) with the bat (God's Word).

In the spiritual realm, an **offensive** use of the Word would be where a skilled believer knows the Word well and is able to recite it immediately to counter any arrow the enemy shoots in his direction. I believe a **defensive** use of the Word would be to know the books of the Bible and their contents well enough (or how to use a concordance, search engines, and Bible apps) so that you can quickly go to any place in scripture and locate a word or phrase to find comfort or to take action. Another defensive posture would be to become so familiar with the Word that you can discern it in the broad sense, to know if someone is speaking the truth.

> It is imperative that believers become skilled at using the Bible to thwart Satan's attacks

Without question, the Word of God is a powerful weapon. It is imperative that believers become skilled at using the Bible to thwart Satan's attacks. Remember that Satan knows the Word of God better than you, and he can twist God's truth into false messages of hope that turn into despair. By studying the Word of God for ourselves, we'll be able to recognize Satan's lies and achieve an advantage against the schemes of the tempter.

GAIN AN ADVANTAGE

In most places of business, people seek an advantage over their competition. Spiritually there isn't a difference, as Satan will utilize anything at his disposal to send a Christian back to the dugout in defeat (unable to be used for kingdom purpose). On the other hand, a Christian is to know the Word of God and utilize it to gain the advantage over the schemes of the evil one, to counter the enemy of darkness and send him away. In baseball, the same approach occurs as teams try to edge out a benefit to gain an advantage over the hitter.

As a Major League catcher for most of the 70s and 80s, I had to stay attuned to certain activities from the opposing team to keep them from using me for their benefit. When a runner from the competing team gets to second base, he has the opportunity to look into a catcher's signs and attempt to relay them to the hitter. Signals can also be relayed from a person viewing a centerfield shot on television to a person in the dugout. In turn, they can relay the signs to a player in the on-deck circle and then to the hitter. There are certain hitters that, when given this advantage, are able to become better hitters.

One of the catcher's roles is to be aware of which strategies are used at what times by which teams, so that any such advantages might be countered. A Christian has the greatest advantage in the Word of God. But the Bible in the hand of a believer can be like a hitter who never gets the bat off his shoulder. Unless you know how to use it, the Word of God stays gift-wrapped.

When I learned to stay within my strengths, I gained an advantage that I didn't have before. By not working to be a home run hitter and therefore concentrating on my ability to hit to right field, I became a skilled hitter. We can use this same idea when approaching our study of the Word of God.

We all have an individual learning style. It is part of God's incredible, unique imprint on us. When we operate within our natural wiring, things just work better. The same holds when it comes to studying the Word of God. It is much easier when we do this through the window of our learning style than trying to conform to someone else's prescribed method. It impacts our motivation to engage. When we interact with scripture organically, it can be a great advantage we can utilize to gain knowledge and understanding of God's Word.

LEARNING STYLE

MOTIVATION

When it comes to doing things out of pure motives, we can fall short. I wish I could say that my flesh nature would allow me to approach the study of God's Word without the discipline of my mind. But I can't. Over the years, my motivation for studying the Bible has changed. I've learned to connect my style of learning to studying the Word.

When I first started reading scripture, my motivation was out of fear and guilt. I imagined this overbearing God looking down with a frown on His face and His arms crossed. Due to my childhood, I was receptive to this form of motivation because I was familiar with these emotions. As I studied more, I began to feel better. The truth of the Word soaked in, so most of my motivation transitioned from fear and guilt to reading because it made me feel good. I had successfully found a new way to gauge my performance. After several years of getting a grip on God's forgiveness and grace and experiencing emotional healing, fear and guilt no longer worked. Since I no longer read out of fear of punishment or disapproval, I fell into a more passive approach to studying the Bible.

To hold myself accountable, I got involved with Bible Studying Fellowship (BSF), which lasted about fifteen years. The rule was that you couldn't participate in your group discussion unless you had done your lesson for that day. The driving motivation then became the need not to be embarrassed because my lesson wasn't done. All along, I felt and knew in my soul that my real motivation should be the desire to know God and to pursue an intimate relationship with Him. Regardless of what drove me, the more I read the Word, the more I came to realize I had an incredible, loving, and gracious God who is patient and understanding of my flesh nature and its impure motives.

The Apostle Paul once said that whether from pure or impure motives, he rejoiced when Christ was preached.[1] This is also true regarding our motivation for studying the Bible. I do not believe God cares so much about what motivates us to engage with His Word as long as we do it. As time goes by and our relationship with Him grows, we gradually approach Him more and more out of a pure motive, to love Him and know Him as He is with no strings attached. My love is so imperfect and so far from God's love that I need whatever help I can get to study the Word.

WHAT IS THE BEST STYLE OF STUDY?

The best style of Bible study will be the one that keeps you engaged with the Word most regularly. No style is better or worse or more or less "spiritual." Style of study is personal. Try them all until you find out what works best for you.

DISCOVERY / SEARCH CONCEPTS

This study style is interest-based. A concept grabs your attention, such as forgiveness or finances. It is more geared toward people who already have a good understanding of the Bible and are on a mission to better define or explore concepts. This book is an example of this style. We are discovering deeper meaning related to the Armor of God. Pursuit of the concept leads the student all over the Bible, connecting pieces of scripture to each other. This is a very independent form of study and not for everyone. Those with high curiosity, who are self-motivated—writers, philosophers, artists, entrepreneurs, inventors … they are often drawn to this method.

Through years of studying the Word, I discovered that this style works well for me when other methods of study lose their appeal. It becomes truly motivating when I can take something through the window by which God has created me. I find that when I am in the process of conceptualizing an idea, I go into "development mode." The adventure of going from point A to point B, discovering how to pull an idea together, and then put it in order makes me come out of my chair with excitement and energy that is hard to match. This book is my latest project in taking a concept from start to finish and putting order to it. In the process of writing, I end up recalling and studying God's Word.

INDUCTIVE

Inductive Bible study may appeal to people who are more technical or methodical. A physician, accountant, teacher, or engineer may find this motivating. The goal is to focus on a specific passage of scripture to determine not just what it says but the intended meaning for the original audience, then how it can be applied today. It begins by focusing on specific details, then broadening the understanding to a more universal principle. The inductive style picks words apart and digs deep into the mind and heart of God to see where a passage fits into the larger scheme of other verses in the chapter. It goes from observation to interpretation to application in a steady, measured process.

ONE-YEAR BIBLE

The One-Year Bible method is attractive to those who appreciate some form of daily structure. There are many great options for this available in print and on apps. Some even have videos to set up each book of the Bible and help you comprehend the main message and themes. Anyone who desires personal accountability in a structured format may find this style works best for them. One clear benefit is that it gets a person into the Word daily, and most allow the freedom to miss some days without too much difficulty catching up.

I want to point out that reading through the Bible with a one-year guide is awesome—as long as you grant yourself grace that it is okay if it takes you longer than a year to do it. The point is to give you a plan with regular portions of scripture outlined for you to get you through the entire Bible. It can, however, easily become a box to check and turn into a performance-based interaction instead of a heart-driven practice. Never let it become that. Let your engagement with God's Word always bring you life, strength, and joy.

STUDY WORKBOOK

Some people enjoy a guided study that gives a portion of scripture to read, offers some commentary or insight, then presents questions for comprehension and reflection. This method is another great way to learn. It is interactive and can provide that "line upon line, precept upon precept"[2] approach. This style of learning is attractive to many people. These texts are usually based on five to six days of study each week, which allows for a day of rest. Most extend from eight to thirteen weeks of study and are often done together with a small group of people for greater accountability.

STRUCTURED CLASS

Most churches have a structured class teaching of the Word. Bible Study Fellowship (BSF), an international non-denominational ministry, has the best-structured format I have encountered for a layperson to learn the Bible. It incorporates four elements of study: class interaction, study notes, study questions, and lecture time. It offers accountability in that one must complete the study questions before they can participate in class dialogue. If a person enjoys social skills, a variety in learning, and wants to truly learn the Bible, this is a great way to go.

Years ago, my secretary told me how much her father-in-law bragged about reading the entire Bible annually year after year. She went on to say he was one of the meanest people she knew. Obviously, his yearly study wasn't doing much to shape his heart. You simply cannot study and meditate on the Word without being changed. *Religious activity of any kind doesn't do much for the soul to reshape a fallen heart.*

It really doesn't matter by which style or method you come to the Word as long as you consistently read the Bible through the lens of a personal relationship with God. Reading, meditating, and memorizing scripture helps you be able to respond to the Holy Spirit when He brings the Word to remembrance for use in time of need.

DISCIPLINES OF STUDY

MEDITATE (DIGEST / WRESTLE)

The next elements of study center around certain learning disciplines because they cause us to slow down and ponder the meaning. Of all the ways to learn the Word, meditation has influenced me the most. It has been my experience and observation that when most read the Bible, they go very quickly—as if there is some award given to the fastest reader of the year. The one-year Bible approach puts people on a structured schedule as if to communicate that staying on schedule and reading every day is more important than anything. This can leave little time to ponder, reflect, and wait quietly to receive from the Lord the deeper essence of a verse or passage. You can reflect on God's Word without formally reading it every day. In these quiet moments of reflection, I have received the greatest nuggets of a deeper nature.

It is also in these quiet moments that intense wrestling occurs as we deal with the conviction that can be brought on by truth in tender places. Meditation will always bring about an array of emotions, from the elation of breakthroughs to the reality of one's fallen nature. But the true gems come to those who will digest and wrestle with God's Word in their pursuit of truth.

MEMORIZING (DISCIPLINE FOR QUICK RECALL)

When approaching memorization of God's Word, one of two things will happen. You will either put a lot of hard work and discipline toward being effective, or because of your natural gifts, you will have an easier attempt at memorizing verses. For example, someone drawn toward acting or drama may be able to memorize scripture more easily.

The only way memorization works for me is through the natural result of meditation. Being ADD, it is very difficult to attend long enough for this discipline to happen by rote as it does with most. But I've gotten better. God, though, seems to have given me an extra measure in meditation that works for me in recalling His Word. What I do remember seems more of an example of the Holy Spirit's ability than mine.

For example, much of this text that incorporates scripture phrases were originally recalled from memory while I was writing. I wrote most of this text first and then went back later and connected the scripture sentences to the actual scripture. I really give credit to the Holy Spirit's ability to recall the scripture phrases used in this book.

Memorizing is one of the best tools a Christian can exercise, but it comes with the price of time and hard work. The results, however, are immeasurable in recalling and targeting a specific verse to a specific need.

PERSONAL PLAYLIST

TARGETING SPECIFIC VERSE TO SPECIFIC NEED

As we move into targeting specific verses to specific needs, think of it like developing your own personal playlist. Most everyone has curated their own music list tailored to personal preferences, memories, or moods. This concept isn't any different. Over time you realize the enemy's strategies and develop your playlist of verses to protect you from those fiery darts. It would be helpful to first look at the direction from which spiritual attacks might occur. Below is a list of four entry points by which the evil one might try to hassle a person.

HEART	Un-reconciled Issues
TESTIMONY	Credibility
MIND	Thought Patterns
RELATIONSHIP WITH CHRIST	Confidence in God

A Major League player goes through a mental transition from the time he leaves the dugout on his way to the on-deck circle before he ends up in the batter's box. This process is geared to allow the player time to develop a plan that he can implement against the pitcher that will result in success. By the time he reaches the batter's box and awaits the first pitch, he is ready for battle. Much thought has gone into this confrontation from both sides of the conflict. Both of the players are extremely skilled and will take turns winning.

In the spiritual sense, we have the winning ticket when approaching the adversary of this age with Christ as our banner. When we choose to access God's power, we have the upper hand. There is no guesswork when it comes to who will win. It does not matter if the ace pitcher from the other team (Satan) is pitching. He is counting on the fact that we will not utilize God's resources but try to go it alone. If pride and arrogance have their way, we will lose.

Over the years, studying God's Word and my relationship with Him has directed me more and more toward the precise use of scripture phrases that apply directly to my need. In this application section, we will tie some loose ends together to narrow the focus toward **easy applications** that push back the enemy influences. We will continue to carry forward some of the messages I wrote in previous chapters as they applied to me. You will have the opportunity to work out your own scenarios. If you can isolate a few situations for yourself, it will make a dramatic difference in leading a victorious Christian life. Let's take each of the above scenarios and give you an example.

TARGET A SPECIFIC VERSE TO A SPECIFIC NEED

DIRECTION OF THE ENEMY'S ATTACK	**YOUR HEART** Un-reconciled Issues
ATTACK 	"You are stupid. You always have been stupid. What makes you think it will be different?"
RESPONSE 	2 CORINTHIANS 5:17 "I have what it takes. I am a new creature in Christ. The old is gone, the new has come."

TARGET A SPECIFIC VERSE TO A SPECIFIC NEED

**DIRECTION OF THE
ENEMY'S ATTACK**

YOUR TESTIMONY
Credibility in the Community

ATTACK

"You hypocrite. Who are
you to think that people
will understand?"

RESPONSE

1 JOHN 1:9
"But God is faithful. Forgiving
those who call upon Him."

TARGET A SPECIFIC VERSE TO A SPECIFIC NEED

**DIRECTION OF THE
ENEMY'S ATTACK**

YOUR MIND
Your Thought Patterns

ATTACK

"Go ahead and do it. A little
fun doesn't hurt anyone.
Do it your way!"

RESPONSE

LUKE 4:8
"It is written: Worship the Lord
your God and serve Him only."

TARGET A SPECIFIC VERSE TO A SPECIFIC NEED

DIRECTION OF THE ENEMY'S ATTACK	YOUR RELATIONSHIP WITH CHRIST Your Postion Before God

ATTACK

"God is really displeased with you. Here comes His wrath!"

RESPONSE

ROMANS 8:1

"There is no condemnation for those who are in Christ. You are deeply loved!"

OUR EDGE

COMMITTED TO TRUTH

There are two ways you can experience victory in sports—one as a bystander or fan of the winning team, and the other as a participant. In the spiritual realm, there are no bystanders nor is there room for the lazy or passive Christian, only committed players. Having been on the sidelines and between the lines, there is something to be said about the exhilaration of being on the front lines and experiencing firsthand the joy of victory. When we join God by utilizing His resources of truth, we are given an edge. Victory is always in reach in this world because our eternity is already secure.

Let me draw upon the '85 World Series one more time. I liken the last four innings of the seventh game of the Series between the St. Louis Cardinals and the Kansas City Royals to the Christian life. As the catcher for the Royals team, we had an eleven-run advantage after five innings of play. Our ace pitcher (Christ) was on the mound, and He had his best stuff. We had the home field advantage (as Christians do), and the score was in our favor (because of the Trinity). The victory (eternity) was in the bag—it was ours to claim, and there was only a short time left to be declared the champions. We played with authority and enthusiasm as the victors (the Christian life) while staying on the alert against a worthy foe (Satan). Finally came the anticipated last pitch (Christ's return) and the joy of the victory in front of our elated fans (angelic beings and the cloud of witnesses).

Being on the winning team is one of life's pleasures that everyone wants to experience. For the Christian, being on God's team is the ultimate winning experience, but the road to Christ-like-ness isn't easy. It takes the discipline of a skilled soldier to know what his weapons are and how to use them.

Following are weapons that God has given us that cut through the enemy and render him defeated. Every believer can easily wield these weapons. The dark forces of this world cannot stand to be in the presence of these tools or bear to hear them used.

It takes the discipline of a skilled soldier to know what his weapons are and how to use them

WEAPONS OF POWER

WEAPON	TYPE OF RESPONSE
WORD OF GOD Your Sword 	ROMANS 8:1 "God's Word says there is no condemnation for those who are in Christ."
PRAYER Freedom to Approach God 	"Heavenly Father, I ask for Your help and direction. Clear a path for me."
WORSHIP Praise and Adoration 	"I will sing songs that affirm who God is the great 'I AM!'"
VERBAL COMMANDS Your Position of Authority 	"In the name of Jesus, you have no power or authority here. Be gone, Satan!"

Becoming skilled at which weapon to use at the appropriate time is a major attribute of the seasoned warrior for Christ. We have crafty and evil enemies in the spirit realm that would like nothing better than to make us ineffective for the Kingdom of God. A deep understanding of God's Word and His other weapons is imperative in experiencing victory against a foe who is so practiced in his strategies and the best spin-master of all time.

ENEMY'S TACTICS

SPIN MASTER

Let me use this opportunity to review the foundational elements by which evil forces use subtleties to deceive the saints.

1. He can move in stealth, not wanting you to know he is there (as a wolf in sheep's clothing).

2. He can act as if he is your friend, someone in whom you can trust (taking you down a path that detours you from God's will).

3. He can use whatever means you give him to turn them against you (such as un-reconciled issues).

4. He can use outside forces to discourage and disappoint (your family, friends, whomever).

5. He can deceive you into thinking that sinful thoughts are harmless (taking you down the river of compromise).

6. He can put a slight spin on the truth that will tempt you toward compromise (resulting in rebellion against God).

Satan is the all-time spin master, and when you come across someone who constantly spins situations to their benefit away from the truth, you are probably looking into the face of evil. It would be wise to turn and get as far away from that person as possible because their path leads to destruction.

SUMMARY

BOOKENDS: TRUTH ANCHORS THE ARMOR

The Sword of the Spirit and Belt of Truth anchor all the other pieces of armor in truth. Without the Word of God, there is no foundation of power by which the others can be effective. The Word is interwoven through the very fabric of every element of each armor piece. Just as there is no Christianity without the Cross and the resurrection, there is no effective way to protect yourself from the evil one without God's resources. Truth and God's Word are central to success.

The Sword of the Spirit comes at the end of the armor verses as the Belt of Truth comes at the beginning, as if to form bookends, keeping all the other pieces in place. As bookends do, they stand firmly erect at each end, keeping order to those books in between. They work to keep the other volumes from moving, slumping over, or falling out of place. In each book waiting to be used, there is valuable information stored that is ordered for that individual text. Together the texts form a series of valuable resources picked by the owner that sits on a shelf as cherished influences in that person's life.

Let's take and put the entire Armor of God together in one possible phrase:

"Weaving the truth throughout your day— using God's resources to hit it back!"

A longer version of this would be:

> **"Weaving the truth throughout your day**
> while understanding the depth of God's love
> through Jesus' work on the Cross,
> being ready to take swift action,
> acknowledging God's power and presence,
> as you discern the attack,
> **using God's resources to hit it back."**

Jesus is the fundamental source for all things. He is God.

- The **Belt of Truth** and the **Sword of the Spirit** stand strongly erect at each end of the armor to anchor its foundation. The two are truth, with Jesus as the author.

- The **Breastplate of Righteousness** connects us to the work of Jesus on the Cross and the advantages of our position in Him through that labor of love.

- The **Ready Shoes**—our feet fitted with the readiness that comes from the Gospel of Peace—take what we have applied from our position in Christ to give us a reason to be ready to join God in service to our fellow man and against our enemy.

- Our **Shield of Faith** beckons us to go deeper with God through life's conflicts and come out as a seasoned soldier.

- The **Helmet of Salvation** calls upon discipline and love to guide our journey in making choices that honor God and bring us closer to the image of Christ.

Together the armor forms an impenetrable shield of guidance and protection for the saint of God to navigate this time of grace here on Earth for spiritual maturity.

Immediately after verse seventeen in Ephesians six, prayer is mentioned three times in verse eighteen and two more times in the next two verses to conclude the armor section. Anytime we see a word in scripture used consecutively in a passage, it is important. We need to stop to see what God is trying to communicate about prayer.

At the end of the armor section, it says to keep on praying about all things. From this, we see that all the armor pieces are bathed in prayer and that we access God's power through prayer. Prayer is the conduit through which the power of God flows. This ties all pieces together.

STEP UP TO THE PLATE

As you find a place to be alone and quiet for this exercise, listen to these two songs and let their words soak into your heart.

- *Simple Gospel* by United Pursuit

- *Voice of God,* Bethel Music by Dante Bowe with Lael and Mitch Wong, produced by Tywan Mack, featuring Steffany Gretzinger and Chandler Moore

Following is a series of questions to help you reflect on how to use the Sword of the Spirit.

1. Have you discovered your best style for studying the word?

    a. Inductive

    b. One Year Bible

    c. Study Workbook

    d. Search/Discovery

    e. Structured Class

    Why is this best for you?

2. Let's review the foundational elements by which evil forces use subtleties to deceive the saints. Which one best describes you?

   a. He can move in stealth, not wanting you to know he is there (as a wolf in sheep's clothing).

   b. He can act as if he is your friend, someone in whom you can trust (taking you down a path that detours you from God's will).

   c. He can use whatever means you give him to turn them against you (such as un-reconciled issues).

   d. He can use outside forces to discourage and disappoint (your family, friends, whomever).

   e. He can deceive you into thinking that sinful thoughts are harmless (taking you down the river of compromise).

   f. He can put a slight spin on the truth that will tempt you toward compromise (resulting in rebellion against God).

"The weapons we fight with are not weapons of the world. On the contrary, they have divine power to demolish strongholds. We demolish arguments and every pretnesion that sets it self up against the knowlede of God, and we take captive every thought to make it obedient to Christ."

2 CORINTHIANS 10:4-5, NIV

TARGET A SPECIFIC VERSE TO A SPECIFIC NEED

DIRECTION OF THE ENEMY'S ATTACK

YOUR HEART
Un-reconciled Issues

ATTACK

RESPONSE

TARGET A SPECIFIC VERSE TO A SPECIFIC NEED

DIRECTION OF THE ENEMY'S ATTACK

YOUR TESTIMONY
Credibility in the Community

ATTACK

RESPONSE

TARGET A SPECIFIC VERSE TO A SPECIFIC NEED

**DIRECTION OF THE
ENEMY'S ATTACK**

YOUR MIND
Your Thought Patterns

ATTACK

RESPONSE

TARGET A SPECIFIC VERSE TO A SPECIFIC NEED

**DIRECTION OF THE
ENEMY'S ATTACK**

**YOUR RELATIONSHIP
WITH CHRIST**
Your Postion Before God

ATTACK

RESPONSE

ENDNOTES

1. Philippians 1:18.
2. Isaiah 28:10, KJV.

Equipped to Win!

KEEP ON PRAYING

SUMMARY

Prayer concludes Paul's verses concerning the Armor of God. This is with good reason. In any military exercise, unfettered communication up the chain of command is vital to the success of any mission. Without prayer—connection with command central—all our weaponry, experience, and skill lose their tactical advantage.

Beyond the obvious military comparison, prayer is vital to intimacy with the Father. It is the method of our conversation and communion with the Triune God that keeps us grounded in our true identity and bathed in His love and care.

We access God's power through prayer. Every piece of armor is secured through prayer—it is at the core of being *Equipped to Win!*

Conclusion
KEEP ON PRAYING

WHAT IS PRAYER?

INTIMACY WITH GOD

Reading God's Word is one of the times we hear from Him as the Spirit intercedes for us and speaks to our heart to make the Word clear. Our prayers are where He hears from us, what He already knows. God uses prayer to bring us closer to Him because we need intimacy with our Creator. He made us as intimate beings that would be drawn toward intimacy with Him. Prayer is our attempt to approach a loving, gracious God who desires to connect that intimacy with Him for our good and His pleasure.

Prayer is a time when we can pour our hearts to our Lord and Savior, who cares deeply about us. It is a safe place to be when we are in the presence of the Abba Father (our Daddy), laying our requests before Him. It is a time when we do not have to wrestle with whether our words are elegantly spoken in a grandiose way. Words do not necessarily even have to be spoken in order for God to hear. No matter what words we say, the Holy Spirit can decipher any of our attempts to talk with God, no matter how inadequate we may feel. Our time alone with God can just be a precious moment to lay our head in the lap of the One who is love to rest.

In any relationship, there is an interaction between two people where an exchange of words crosses back and forth from one to the other. One difficulty many people have with prayer is that they can't audibly hear back from God but must discern His response in their spirit. This process of discernment is difficult for many because it requires that we become a student with abandonment to know God.

A response from the Holy One may come later as we read His Word as the Holy Spirit confirms to us God's answer. God's response may come through dialogue with another person, yet again, being brought to our attention by the Spirit. Confirmation may come in our quiet time with God as something is resolved through quietness and peace that words cannot communicate. It may come through nature or music. Art or a book. He is not limited, and He will speak to you through a means you can comprehend. Be assured that God's responses will always align with His Word and require the Holy Spirit's help to discern.

All prayers require a person to know by faith that God is there and He is listening. In His timing, which is always best for us, He will respond with the best scenario. Even though we cannot hear Him in the same manner that we hear a friend or family member, we can learn to receive from Him.

WHY IS PRAYER IMPORTANT?

PRAYER IS OUR LIFELINE

A friend's story moved me years ago as he communicated the relationship between the firehouse to firemen. When a group of firemen goes into a fire, they depend upon the water fed through the hose for survival. The hose and the water running through it become their lifeline. Without the hose (prayer), the water (Jesus) cannot be fed to the blaze (requests). This source of power battles against the inferno (Satan). The consistent feeding of the water continually gives them the ability to have life. The receiving of water thwarts the fire's ability to spread chaos and cause destruction.

God sets up prayer as the means by which we get quiet before Him. Prayer is our conduit to receive power to operate a godly life. Prayer is to the Christian as fuel is to an engine, as water is to a fish, as blood is to the body, as air is to a tire, as money is to the ability to purchase goods, as sperm and an egg are to the development of a baby. Because God has set it up this way, there will be very little done by God without prayer. It is His system.

Prayer isn't listed as part of the armor pieces in the Ephesians passage, and it comes at the back end of the list, but that doesn't diminish its importance in adding power and authority. Prayer is probably the first thing we should go to when stuff happens. The application of armor results in an overarching victorious godly life; prayer serves to cover the armor pieces while pursuing immediate attention from the Father. I have come to believe those fitted in the Armor of God and immersed in prayer are true warriors for God, able to stand against the hardest attacks.

It took me eight years into my walk with the Lord before I reached out to a group to pray. My experience tells me I haven't been the only one to wait so long to have others pray with and for them.

One fear MLB players share is that they may draw attention to themselves in the post-season that will never be forgotten. Remember Billy Buckner in the 1986 World Series when he let the ball go between his legs? It was 18 years later, in 2004, after the Red Sox won the World Series before the Boston Globe stated that Red Sox fans had finally forgiven Buckner. You get the picture. Messing up under the big lights of post-season is a no-no.

In 1985 I moved to develop a life board of directors consisting of eight family members and close friends. It was this group that I reached out to and asked them to pray for me in the post-season. I was honest with an appeal to pray that I have a great post-season with no mishaps that drew attention. As I had them pray, the result was that I had a great post-season. I didn't have them pray for a championship, but it was an added bonus to the year. The most spiritual moment during the post-season due to prayer went like this:

The Kansas City Royals were the first team in MLB history to come from behind, down three games to one, and win. We had just won game five in Kansas City against the Toronto Blue Jays. We had a charter flight to Toronto right after the game with an off day the next day.

The eastern skies were full of beautiful thunderheads showing off their magnificent light show as the plane made its way northeast. The combination of lightning and the sun's reflection off the climbing clouds was unmatched from previous flights. The display of power was awesome.

As I was looking out my window, in my spirit, I heard, "Something wonderful is going to happen!" It was almost audible as the strength of the message permeated my soul. The message caused me to tear up in anticipation. It was a moment like Kevin Costner had in the movie *Field of Dreams* when he heard, "If you build it, they will come."

Janet looked over at me and asked, "What's going on, Jim?"

I told her about the message. She responded with enthusiasm and sat back in her seat. It was strange to tear up on a team flight with all the families on board. I pressed back in my seat as the tears flowed. *Now what and when was the next thing to happen?*

We spent a great off day in the beautiful Toronto city as the girls shopped and the guys went to the field for practice. Nothing unusual happened that day or the next with game six as we won it to go to game seven. Nothing had happened that would confirm my message from the plane ride.

We were in the sixth inning of game seven with a 2-1 lead when the message again spoke loud to me. There were runners at first and second, with Steve Balboni hitting as I entered the on-deck circle. All of a sudden, I heard, "This is the moment!" I looked around my shoulder to see if anyone was speaking to me, but obviously, no one was there but a crowd of people 20 feet away in the stands.

Steve Balboni was working the count off Toronto pitcher Dave Steib when again I heard, "Get ready, the bases will be loaded." That was the last message I heard until I stepped into the batter's box to hit.

I had been processing my plate appearance while in the on-deck circle and thought Steib would probably start me off with a slider. Sure enough, the first pitch was a slider but too low to hit. What happened next was an out-of-body experience.

A hitter is trained to only swing at a pitch he is anticipating to be thrown until he has two strikes. I was again looking at a slider for the second pitch. As Steib began his wind-up and pitch, it was a fastball. Against all training, my hands exploded at the ball, sending it high toward the right-field line. My body went into slow motion as I left the batter's box, watching Jesse Barfield in pursuit in right field. As he headed back to the fence and leaped high against the ten-foot wall, the ball hit off the top of the fence. If it had gone over, it would be a grand slam—but it landed in play. My body came out of slow motion, and I trotted into third base with a three-run triple. We were now leading 5-1 and would go on to advance to the World Series.

The moment was an act of destiny. Planned long ago by the Creator of all things. It's like I couldn't have messed it up. He wanted me to participate in something wonderful with Him according to my gift mix. He wanted me to see the power of prayer.

I have zero doubt in my mind that the Holy Spirit orchestrated that moment. Prayer matters! I believe if it wasn't for the prayers of others during the playoffs, the experience of the message and forthcoming triple might not have happened.

— • ● • —

Prayer aligns us with the Father in doing what He is up to doing.

— • ● • —

It's powerful and effective when we line up with His will. He is a faithful God who loves to do things cooperating with the natural gifts and talents He gave us.

STEP UP TO THE PLATE

As you find a place to be alone and quiet for this exercise, listen to these two songs and let their words soak into your heart.

- *Run to the Father,* Capitol Christian Music Group, by Cody Carnes with Matt Maher and Ran Matthew Jackson

- *Lord I Need You*, Capitol Christian Music Group, by Daniel Carson, Matt Maher, Christy Nockels, Jesse Reeves, Kristian Stanfill

HOW DO I EXERCISE PRAYER?

One morning, I got a prayer request from a friend whose father was in the hospital. The appeal read, "Let's be praying for Bill; he's in the hospital. At this point in my walk with God, I felt an uneasiness about responding effectively to this plea because I didn't have enough information about the man. Was he old and dying? Did I need to pray for comfort in his last days? And if so, did I need to pray for his salvation? Was it associated with an illness that was a puzzle to doctors? Did I need to request wisdom for the medical staff? Was the trip to the hospital the result of a severe accident that required surgery? Did I need to lift to the Lord the physician's accurate use of his hands? Or was it something that wasn't serious and required that I just plea for a speedy recovery?

This scenario prompted me to ask several more questions. Is the exercise of prayer for God, or is it for us? What is the purpose of focused prayers, or is there a need for us to be so accurate? Surely, God knows the need and can respond to our inadequacy, uncertainty, or laziness in prayer. Do precise prayers cause us to clarify, for ourselves and not God, what we actually want God to do? And by doing so, does it not help us to more directly see God's hand at work? Or maybe prayer is a process by which we line up our requests to God's will?

For many, prayer is very casual, as if any prayer that one prays, God will respond. There is only One God. Any prayer spoken outside of our relationship with God falls on deaf ears. Any prayer, other than those spoken through Christ the door to the Father, are only religious acts motivated to make us feel better. These prayers quickly pass with no real sustenance. Or God, in His great mercy, will reach out in His supernatural way to respond to draw an unbelieving heart closer to Him.

It is interesting how we can be so precise with some lists and requirements—a grocery list, to-do list, birthday and anniversary list, and a Christmas list. When my kids were growing up, they never prepared a Christmas list that was broad or vague like, "Oh dad, it's okay, just give me whatever you think is best," or "Just go into Toys R Us and pick up a couple of things." No, the kid's lists were very detailed and down to the model numbers, so I would not fail them. They were specific, so I would be able to produce exactly what they asked for. Isn't this what our prayers should include?

My children made specific requests to a good father who delighted in blessing them from his abundance.

As I got older and people asked me for a Christmas list, I would seldom come up with one. It just wasn't important to me anymore, or I didn't want to put forth the effort to put a list together. It just wasn't a priority for me because I didn't see the value. Let this never be with prayer!

Over the years, my study of God's Word and my relationship with Him have directed me more and more toward praying precise prayers that apply directly to the need. I have discovered that, much like we give more grace to a child when they are growing up but require more of them as adults, so it is in our relationship with the Lord and when it comes to our prayer life.

Prayer is not something that we are to do passively. It takes thought and reverence when we attempt to approach the Holy One, and in this intimate time, we need to be prepared to wrestle with the words that come out of our mouth or the words we hear. Prayer is an awesome privilege reserved for only an elite group of priests in Old Testament times. But in New Testament times, Jesus has become our High Priest, and all believers are now part of the priesthood. We have the incredible opportunity to approach God on our knees with the assurance that He will hear us and respond. Reflect now:

1. How is your prayer life? Do you feel an intimate exchange between you and your Father, or do you struggle with being overly formal or overly casual?

2. How do you hear God? In what ways does He speak to you that you most recognize the message is coming from Him?

3. Pause right now and get alone with God in quietness. Let your heart receive His love and respond in wonder.

Summary

PUT ON YOUR ARMOR

"Finally, be strong in the Lord and in His mighty power.

Put on the **FULL ARMOR OF GOD**, so that you can take your stand against the devil's schemes.

For our struggle is not against flesh and blood, but against the rulers, against the authorities, against the powers of this dark world and against the spiritual forces of evil in the heavenly realms.

Therefore, put on the full armor of God, so that when the day of evil comes, you may be able to **STAND YOUR GROUND**, and after you have done everything, to stand.

Stand firm then, with the **BELT OF TRUTH** buckled around your waist, with the **BREASTPLATE OF RIGHTEOUNSESS** in place, and with your feet fitted with readiness that comes from the Gospel of Peace (**READY SHOES**).

In addition to all this, take up the **SHIELD OF FAITH**, with which you can extinguish all the flaming arrows of the evil one.

Take the **HELMET OF SALVATION** and the **SWORD OF THE SPIRIT**, which is the Word of God.

And pray in the Spirit on all occassion with all kinds of prayers and requests. With this in mind, be alert and **ALWAYS KEEP ON PRAYING** for all the Lord's people."

EPHESIANS 6:10-18, NIV

LET'S REVIEW

BELT OF TRUTH—SET FREE

- Jesus is our starting place and the foundation for all truth.
- Truth holds together all the pieces of armor.
- I put on the Belt of Truth by pursuing intimacy with the Father—shooting straight with Jesus.

THIS IS A BATTLE FOR TRUTH

- TRUTH ZONE—Intimacy with God kindles a passionate pursuit of truth.

BREASTPLATE OF RIGHTEOUSNESS—HEART RESCUE

- Our identity and position in Christ are precious, and they must be guarded.
- Once wounded, it is easy to wrap lies around our identity that seem like the truth. The Breastplate of Righteousness is there not only to shield us from the enemy's fiery darts (lies), but also to provide a place of safety and refuge so our wounds can heal as we pursue the path of forgiveness that leads to peace.
- When I absorb God's deep love, I put on the Breastplate of Righteousness. This piece of armor protects my heart and reminds me that I am forgiven, approved, accepted, and renewed.

THIS IS A BATTLE FOR IDENTITY (SIGNIFICANCE)

- "IN CHRIST" ZONE—We come to the place where we believe and trust who we <u>already are</u> in Christ Jesus.

READY SHOES—OUR TESTIMONY

- When our feet are fitted with the readiness that comes from the Gospel of peace, we are able to stand our ground—have solid footing—with God.

- The Ready Shoes relate to our ability to experience God and share the Good News about Him with others. When we wear them, we unleash the power of our testimony.

- I put on the Ready Shoes when I become grounded in the Word of God, standing on a firm foundation, I am in a state of readiness to join God in carrying out the Great Commission as I walk out my faith authentically.

THIS IS A BATTLE FOR READINESS

- READINESS ZONE—Because I am aware of His presence, I am surrounded by grace. I am attentive to God-encounters.

SHIELD OF FAITH—UNYIELDING BELIEF

- The Shield of Faith in place indicates that it is in God we trust.

- Faith in God delivers hope to our hearts—it is His goodness, not our abilities, that shields and protects us from falling apart in difficult circumstances.

- I put on the Shield of Faith when I say to God, "I believe; help me with my unbelief."

THIS IS A BATTLE FOR FAITH OVER FEAR

- KNOWING ZONE—Trust in God's goodness and sovereignty is the pathway to knowing, even when we do not understand.

HELMET OF SALVATION—CHOOSING RIGHT

- Wearing the Helmet of Salvation indicates you have engaged in the battle to have a mind like Christ.

- Our mind is where we exercise free will. Our life is the sum of our choices, and great choices require that we renew our minds with the washing of the water of the Word and make decisions fully aware of the sacrifice Christ made for our salvation.

- I put on the Helmet of Salvation when I manage my thoughts and choose to do what Jesus would do (WWJD).

THIS IS A BATTLE FOR A DISCIPLINED MIND

- RIGHT CHOICE ZONE—I can access God's wisdom by asking, "Lord, what is this about?" and "What do You want me to do?"

SWORD OF THE SPIRIT—OUR EDGE

- Wielding the Sword of the Spirit allows us to deploy a strategic strike against the enemy with God's Word.

- More than just knowing the Word of God, using the Sword of the Spirit is the active engagement of a believer with the Word. It indicates we have a deeper understanding and helps us gain an advantage over the schemes of the evil one.

- I wield the Sword of the Spirit when I target specific verses to specific needs. I come into agreement with the principles and promises of God found in His Word.

THIS IS A BATTLE FOR STRATEGIC STRIKES

- SPECIAL OPS ZONE—I use strategy and beat the enemy with targeted scriptures that strike true.

KEEP PRAYING IN THE SPIRIT—OUR POWER

- Prayer is a time when we can pour our hearts to our Lord and Savior, who cares deeply about us. It is a safe place to be when we are in the presence of the Abba Father (our Daddy), laying our requests before Him.

- All prayers require a person to know by faith that God is there and He is listening. In His timing, which is always best for us, He will respond.

- We access God's power through prayer. Every piece of armor is secured through prayer.

THIS IS A BATTLE FOR ALIGNMENT WITH THE SPIRIT

- PRAYER ZONE—I communicate freely with the Spirit as He intercedes for me and helps me to pray.

HEARING GOD'S VOICE

The following is used with permission from Fellowship of the Sword. It is an exercise from Quest Men's Event. To learn more, please visit thequestlife.com.

GOD **THE GOOD SHEPHERD**	SATAN **THE THIEF**	OURSELVES **THE SHEEP**
Loves and woos	Drives and forces	Desires Attention
Encourages	Intimidates, demands, and threatens	Has unreasonable expectations
Gives clear, specific instructions	Exaggerates, gives vague, confusing instructions	Analyzes all instructions
Calls us by name, personal	Uses derogatory, negative speech	Is self-promoting or self-demeaning
Speaks truth because He values you	Lies, attacks, devalues	Manipulates and controls
Convicts of sin and offers forgiveness	Condemns, rejects, blames	Self-protects and justifies actions
Speaks in supernatural ways	Uses magic, tricks, spells, sensationalism	Uses reason and logic

GOD	SATAN	OURSELVES
THE GOOD SHEPHERD	**THE THIEF**	**THE SHEEP**
Offers hope and strength	Instills fear and doubt	Depends on self and pride
Stretches you	Limits what you can do	Limits you to natural abilities
Doesn't compare you to others	Forces comparison	Compares you to others
Ample provision	Never enough	Is materialistic, self-sufficient
Wants you to trust God only	Wants you to trust anything but God	Wants you to trust yourself
Wants all the glory!	Wants all the glory!	Wants all the glory!

This Hearing God Chart is the intellectual property of Fellowship of the Sword Ministries. © 2002-2022 by Richard Henderson. All Rights Reserved. It has been used by permission and my not be reproduced in whole or in part in any way without written permission of Fellowship of the Sword.

"With practical advice, Jim and Janet share how to best parent a child in sports, eliminate the possible frustrations and disappointments, and bring out the best in a sports experience."

DAVE DRAVECKY, PRESIDENT, OUTREACH OF HOPE

"*How to Win at Sports Parenting* puts kids and sports into the proper context for success—personal success and family success."

RICHARD SCHULTZ, EXECUTIVE DIRECTOR UNITED STATES OLYMPIC COMITTEE

SPORTS IS MORE THAN JUST A GAME

Discover how to help your children ...

- **Enjoy to the fullest the sports they play**

- **Learn valuable sports-to-life-lessons**

- **Deal with game-day emotions in a healthy manner**

- **Develop crucial skills they will use the rest of their lives**

Drawing from a rich background in sports, parenting, and family development, Jim Sundberg and his wife, Janet, teach that the sports experience can provide unique opportunities for kids to deal with emotions and develop the skills necessary for healthy, life-enhancing, interaction with others. But for this to happen, moms and dads need a practical plan.

The Sundbergs will help you build that plan by showing you *How to Win at Sports Parenting.*

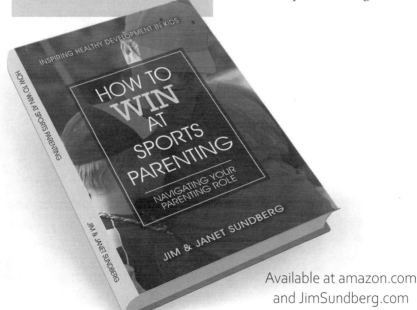

INSPIRING HEALTHY DEVELOPMENT IN KIDS

HOW TO WIN AT SPORTS PARENTING

HOW TO
WIN
AT
SPORTS
PARENTING

NAVIGATING YOUR PARENTING ROLE

JIM & JANET SUNDBERG

Available at amazon.com
and JimSundberg.com

LEGACY *Playbook*

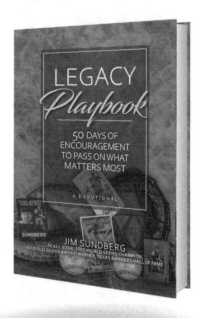

Life is a long journey filled with strikes, fouls, and curveballs, so we could all use some encouragement along the way. In this 50-Day Devotional, Texas Ranger Hall of Famer Jim Sundberg shares personal stories from his 16-year Major League Baseball career. Many are humorous and give a rare behind-the-scenes look at events and personalities around the dugout. Some are gripping, such as the loss of their first daughter and grappling with childhood abuse that led to emotional dysfunction and a battle with depression. Through them all, Jim candidly shares his quest to know the God who created him and fashioned him to play baseball.

This LEGACY PLAYBOOK offers a daily short story from Jim, a promise from Scripture, a song, a few questions for mindful reflection, then a prompt to journal a prayer and write down what you hear the Father saying back to you. At the conclusion of each chapter, there is an invitation to reflect on the chapter's theme, and through that lens of legacy, determine what matters most to you.

Available at amazon.com
and JimSundberg.com